D0578706

PRIDE

The LGBTQ+ Rights Movement

PR

The LGBTQ+ Rights Movement

A PHOTOGRAPHIC JOURNEY

Written & Edited by CHRISTOPHER MEASOM

Personal **R**ights **I**n **D**efense and **E**ducation

Personal Rights in Defense and Education (PRIDE) was a radical gay political organization founded by Steve Ginsburg in 1966 to alter the relationship between the police and the gay community and to provide social events outside of the bar scene. There was a bridge club, bowling team, hiking club, and discussion group, and they held dances. They also created a legal defense fund and were key in organizing the first gay demonstration against police brutality at the Black Cat Bar, which paved the way for gay political groups like the Gay Liberation Front, ACT UP, and the Radical Faeries. PRIDE's monthly single-page newsletter evolved into *The Advocate*, the nation's longest-running gay news publication.

An Imprint of Sterling Publishing Co., Inc.
1166 Avenue of the Americas
New York, NY 10036

ISBN: 978-1-4549-3655-8

Distributed in Canada by Sterling Publishing Co., Inc.
c/o Canadian Manda Group, 664 Annette Street
Toronto, Ontario M6S 2C8, Canada
Distributed in the United Kingdom by GMC Distribution Services
Castle Place, 166 High Street, Lewes, East Sussex BN7 1XU, England
Distributed in Australia by NewSouth Books
45 Beach Street, Coogee, NSW 2034, Australia

For information about custom editions, special sales, and premium and corporate purchases, please contact Sterling Special Sales at 800-805-5489 or specialsales@sterlingpublishing.com.

Manufactured in Canada

2 4 6 8 1 0 9 7 5 3 1

sterlingpublishing.com

Interior design by Timothy Shaner, NightandDayDesign.biz

Cover design by Elizabeth Mihaltse Lindy

Picture Credits – see page 168

CONTENTS

GAY IS A
STONEWALL MEANS FIGHT BACK! SMASH GAY OPPRESSION!
GAY CAUCUS-
AGAINST WAR & FASCISM
POLICE DEPT.

INTRODUCTION

MAKING SPACE

"We were dancing, my lover and I, and the next thing we know, the lights came on and . . . hey, we're being raided. Queens started being filed out and put into police cars. Guns had been drawn, Molotov cocktails were flying. And I'm like, 'Oh, my God, the revolution is here—thank God!'"

So said Sylvia Rivera about that fateful night in June 1969 as the police raided a small and ordinary bar on Christopher Street in Greenwich Village called the Stonewall Inn. This particular raid—one of perhaps thousands of similar routine assaults that had happened before—sparked the LGBTQ+ rights movement.

Here we are a half century later, the perfect occasion to pause and take a look back to see just how far we've traveled—and celebrate in wonder. "The world was so different then," said human rights activist and artist Tommy Lanigan-Schmidt during a June 4, 2007 panel discussion at the Stonewall Inn. "Gay people were scheduled for nonexistence. In other words, we were supposed to have no reality called 'gay,' 'homosexual,' except to be in a mental institution getting shock treatments or getting fired from a job."

The brawl at Stonewall was unexpected, to say the least. "The police got the shock of their lives when those queens came out of that bar and pulled off their wigs and went after them," recalled Stormé DeLarvarie, who, rumor has it, threw the first punch that night. "I knew sooner or later people were going to get the same attitude that I had. They had just pushed once too often."

Opposite: Christopher Street Liberation Day march, June 1972.

And looking back fifty years before Stonewall, the roots of the movement can be seen taking hold.

"How ya gonna keep 'em down on the farm after they've seen Paree?" a popular song asked in 1919 about World War I's returning doughboys. It continued, "How ya gonna keep 'em away from Broadway, jazzin' around and painting the town?" Well, as it happens, the vets—along with many black Southerners fleeing the injustices of Jim Crow—left the farm in droves for city life in the 1920s, and in place of cows and corn they cultivated a bohemian subculture. There were speakeasies, gay parties, and drag balls along with the words of Radclyffe Hall, Vita Sackville-West, and Noël Coward—these were the early seeds of the gay rights movement. "Girls were girls and boys were boys when I was a tot, now we don't know who is who or even what's what," observed another popular song of the era. And culture, just a tiny bit, shifted.

Progress stepped up as the extraordinary upheavals of World War II led to a growing confluence of human rights awakening and cultural change. Women had built ships and joined the army and began to see independence as a viable life choice. Black soldiers returned from overseas wondering why the rights they'd been fighting for didn't apply to them at home. Many gay people, meanwhile, had discovered themselves (and others!). They settled in cities (opting for freedom over small-town repression), and suddenly, visible gay communities appeared and organizations formed.

But as homophiles gingerly opened their closet doors, tremendous backlash followed. Conformity ruled the day, and gay people were targeted with laws specifically meant to repress. "In the 1950s . . . California's Alcoholic Beverage Control Board ruled that acts of touching, women wearing mannish attire, and men with limp wrists, high-pitched voices, and/or tight clothing were evidence of a bar's 'dubious character' and grounds for closing it," wrote a group of scholars about the history of antigay discrimination in an amicus brief for a same-sex marriage case in 2014. New York State outlawed plays with gay or lesbian characters, the gay political magazine *One* was banned as obscene, and in 1950, the US Senate declared homosexuals to be "generally unsuitable" for employment in the federal government. Harassment, injustice, and threats were everywhere if you were queer.

And yet, as Sylvia Rivera had long been hoping that summer night in 1969, as she danced with her lover at the Stonewall Inn, rebellion was brewing.

There were many small, spur-of-the-moment uprisings in the 1960s (see pages 59–60). But it was the Christopher Street Gay Liberation Day march in 1970, marking the first anniversary of Stonewall—the first pride parade—that was almost more important than the uprising itself. "Just please let there be more than ten of us," gay rights activist Doric Wilson said about that day in the 2011 documentary *Stonewall Uprising*. "We were about 100, 120 people and there were people lining the sidewalks ahead of us to watch us go by, gay people, mainly." Activist and fellow marcher Jerry Hoose added, "We were scared but as we were going up Sixth Avenue, it kept growing." Doric continued, "And I looked back and there were about 2,000 people behind us . . . and Vito [Russo] and I walked the rest of the whole thing with tears running down our face."

"Keep your heads up!" Hoose shouted to his fellow marchers, "You're not in a dark bar anymore, but in the sunshine." It was a tipping point.

Above: An image that has come to be synonymous with the Compton's Cafeteria riot in San Francisco in 1966 is actually an image documenting a protest by Gay Guerilla Theater in San Francisco, outside the Beaux Arts Ball fundraiser, on Halloween, 1969.

NATIONAL COMING OUT DAY...
©K.Haring 88
OCTOBER 11-1988
NATIONAL GAY RIGHTS ADVOCATES

Where pre-Stonewall socializing and organizing and pushing was slow and deliberately conservative (out of necessity), post-Stonewall activism—inspired by the civil rights and women's lib movements and anti–Vietnam War protests—was far more aggressive. Times had changed, and the 1970s gay liberationist's chant "Hey, hey, what d'ya say? Try it once the other way!" was more likely to be met with a chuckle (and maybe even consideration) than with handcuffs. Even the AIDS crisis that followed (seemingly bringing the movement to a screeching halt) led, in retrospect, to a remarkable push forward. The visible, swift, and devastating disease forced gay men out of the closet in droves, making it clear to people that homosexuals were not criminals or deviants but our most cherished friends and family members.

As a result of these decades of action, counterpunches, setbacks, and progress, the movement's legacy is written in our laws, walks the halls of Congress, and flickers on movie screens. We see its impact in new FDA drug protocols, the repeal of the discriminatory "Don't Ask, Don't Tell" military policy, and the right to marry as the law of the land. Openly gay, lesbian, bisexual, and transgender people have been elected to the US Senate and House of Representatives. And the 2019 Oscars® celebrated an abundance of characters from the silver screen—from an eighteenth-century British monarch to a black musician traveling through the 1960s' South—whose sexuality was not the focus of the films. However much the LGBTQ+ acronym may evolve, the movement has made strides that have reshaped society—and that generations can build upon.

So what of the future? Will it be, as journalist Andrew Sullivan said in a 2005 *New Republic* essay, that "the distinction between gay and straight culture will become so blurred, so fractured, and so intermingled that it may become more helpful not to examine them separately at all"? Will the idea that sexuality runs along a broad spectrum take hold in a way that ensures we make space for those who are different from us? Yes, there is much work to be done. But if the past century of movement toward pride, rights, and dignity is any indication, the possibilities for the next hundred years are as rich and diverse as, well, human sexuality.

Opposite: Poster by Keith Haring for the first National Coming Out Day, 1988.

PART 1
WE'RE HERE . . .

DON'T GO IN THE WATER, DAUGHTER

JULIAN ELTINGE'S
BATHING SONG

THE WORLD OF NIGHT (1920–1930)

The 1920s came in with a roar. Out went the morals and fashions of the nineteenth century and in came everything modern: telephones, cars, talking pictures, radio, short skirts, even people flying across the ocean. Following World War I, a sense of freedom and prosperity was beginning to take root. Women could finally vote and a new, more industrial economy boomed. And so the cities filled—many newcomers being black Southerners escaping Jim Crow laws—and a bohemian subculture emerged.

Up in Harlem there were speakeasies, rent parties, and places like Club Hot-Cha and Gladys' Clam House, where the spectrum of human sexuality—along with jazz and bootleg alcohol—was on display. As historian Henry Louis Gates Jr. described it, the Harlem Renaissance "was surely as gay as it was black."

Downtown there was Greenwich Village, a neighborhood of Irish and Italian immigrants that, due to the cheap rents, was attracting "people with taste, but no money—artists, writers, and poorly paid professional people," wrote Caroline Ware in *Greenwich Village, 1920–1930* (1963). In other words, freethinkers.

And in the middle there was Mae West, who was arrested in 1926 for her Broadway play *Sex*, which—far ahead of her time—she wrote, directed, and starred in. Two years later she staged *two* plays about cross-dressing, specifically casting gay men, a practice forbidden by union rules at the time. *The Drag* (subtitled *A Homosexual Comedy in Three Acts*) dealt with the foibles of a closeted gay socialite, and *The Pleasure Man* didn't quite last three performances (it was raided twice by the police).

The public was obviously curious, since the Mae West shows played to packed houses and Harlem was always hopping, and though this exploration and boundary pushing was mostly happening after dark and in the more freethinking enclaves of New York, it was also in the air.

Previous pages: Cross-dressing partygoers, c. 1930. **Opposite**: Sheet music from the 1911 Broadway musical *The Fascinating Widow*, featuring the hugely popular cross-dressing vaudeville and silent film star Julian Eltinge. Strikingly beautiful, he mesmerized audiences with his gender-illusion performances nationwide, garnering many marriage proposals from unsuspecting men.

In Britain, Radclyffe Hall's 1928 novel *The Well of Loneliness,* about a well-heeled lesbian facing society's rejection, had good reviews and great sales (which only got better after an editorial calling it "immoral" appeared in the *Sunday Express*). Out west in Hollywood—which was quickly becoming storyteller to the world—box office heartthrob William Haines lived openly with his partner, James Shields. And in the Midwest during the 1920s, America's first gay organization was born.

In 1924, German immigrant and mild-mannered Chicago postal worker Henry Gerber—who was familiar with the work of sexologist Magnus Hirschfeld ("Germany's Einstein of Sex")—formed a group called the Society for Human Rights to "promote and protect the interests of people who by reasons of mental and physical abnormalities [homosexuals] are abused and hindered in the legal pursuit of happiness."

And then there was Alan Hart from rural Kansas, who just never felt right wearing dresses and playing with dolls as a child. According to a neighbor's recollection printed in the *Halls Summit News* in 1921, he "hated traditional girl tasks, preferring farm work with the menfolk instead." In 1918, at the age of twenty-seven, Hart underwent medical transition and lived the rest of his life as a man.

"Sister is busy learning to shave,
Brother just loves his permanent wave.
It's hard to tell 'em apart today,
Knickers and trousers baggy and wide,
Nobody knows who's walking inside."

—Lyrics from "Masculine Women, Feminine Men"
by Edgar Leslie/James V. Monaco, 1926

Yes—there were stumbles. Mae West's shows were closed and she went to jail, Henry Gerber got only six men to join his organization before he was arrested for being gay (police planted a powder puff as evidence) and lost his job, and William Haines was fired from MGM. But Alan Hart was a successful doctor, married twice, and got a master's degree—his second—from Yale in the 1940s.

More importantly, however, consciousness had been raised and ideas had been born. People were interested in (if not quite ready to accept) pansexuality. And though there would be a lull in LGBTQ+ advances during the Great Depression, the dual forces of culture and organization were simmering around the edges of society.

Opposite: Alla Nazimova in a publicity shot from the 1923 silent film *Salomé*, adapted from Oscar Wilde's play. Hollywood legend has it that star and producer Nazimova demanded that the entire cast be composed of gay or bisexual actors in homage to Wilde. Nazimova wielded considerable influence and power in Hollywood at the time and was rumored to be involved in numerous lesbian affairs. Legend also has it that she coined the phrase "sewing circle" as code referring to lesbian or bisexual actresses. Nazimova lived with actress and theatrical benefactor (and godmother to future first lady Nancy Reagan) Glesca Marshall from 1929 until Nazimova's death in 1945.

GLENROY TENBY

ARROW COLLARS

are favored by men who are fam
who, in their dress, impart an imp

There is an ARROW COLLAR for every taste, every face and every occasion. 15c each 2 for 25c

Send for PROPER DRESS and EVENING ATTIRE, two good books on fashion, by an authority.

DORSET ARCANUM MARGATE

ND CLUETT SHIRTS

ar with the trend of fashion, and
ssion of distinguished individuality.

Enough of the shirt appears to show that it is a color-fast perfectly fitting CLUETT. $1.50 and up

CLUETT, PEABODY & COMPANY, Makers, 457 River Street, Troy, N. Y.

Previous pages and **Opposite**: The wildly popular Arrow Collar Man was the creation of famed illustrator J. C. Leyendecker and was modeled on his partner of fifty years, Charles Beach. The campaign for shirts and detachable shirt collars ran from 1905 to 1931, but Leyendecker's work, often showing beautiful men gazing at each other, also appeared on over four hundred magazine covers and in newspapers across the world. His strongly homoerotic images were so influential that they are referenced in the Irving Berlin song "Puttin' on the Ritz" and Cole Porter's "You're the Top," and they were copied by Leyendecker's admirer Norman Rockwell. **Above**: Facing the camera, Violet Oakley (left), Jessie Willcox Smith (right), and Elizabeth Shippen Green, also known as the Red Rose Girls. This group of women artists from Philadelphia active in the early 1900s, lived and worked together in a nontraditional, women-only household along with their housekeeper, Henrietta Cozens. "They were independent yet feminine, feminine and maternal yet childless, attractive yet without beaus, and financially successful without male providers," wrote scholar Charlotte Herzog about the women. Oakley considered herself the "man of the house."

Above: Actor William "Billy" Haines in a still from the 1929 film *Speedway.* Haines's acting career was cut short in the 1930s due to his refusal to deny his sexuality. When movie mogul Louis B. Mayer suggested Haines get married (to a woman), he said, "I'm already married." He quit acting in 1935 and started a successful interior design business with his life partner, Jimmie Shields. Good friend and interior design client Joan Crawford described the men as "the happiest married couple in Hollywood." **Right**: Marguerite Radclyffe Hall (right) was a prizewinning writer whose novel *The Well of Loneliness* was originally banned in Britain for its sympathetic approach to lesbianism. She is pictured here in 1927 with Lady Una Troubridge, whom she lived with for more than two decades. Early in their relationship, Troubridge wrote in her diary, "I could not, having come to know her, imagine life without her."

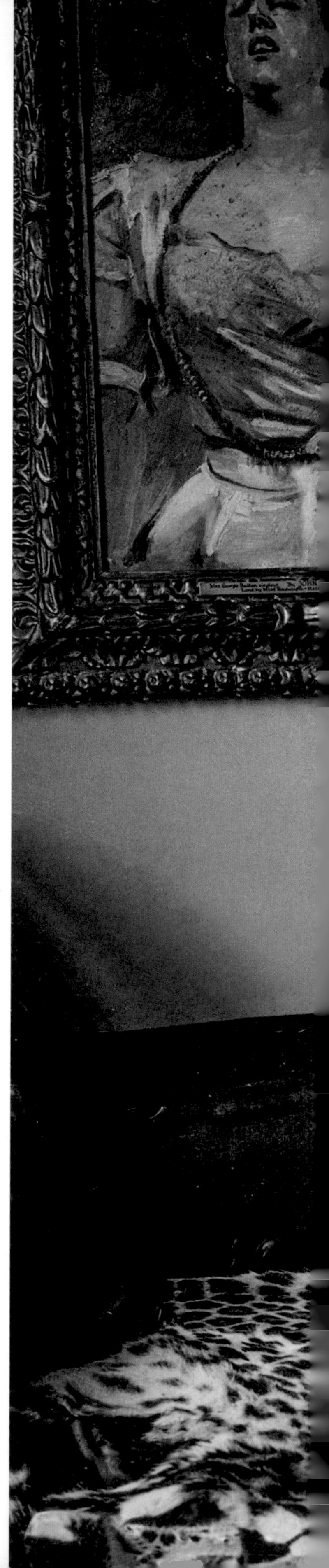

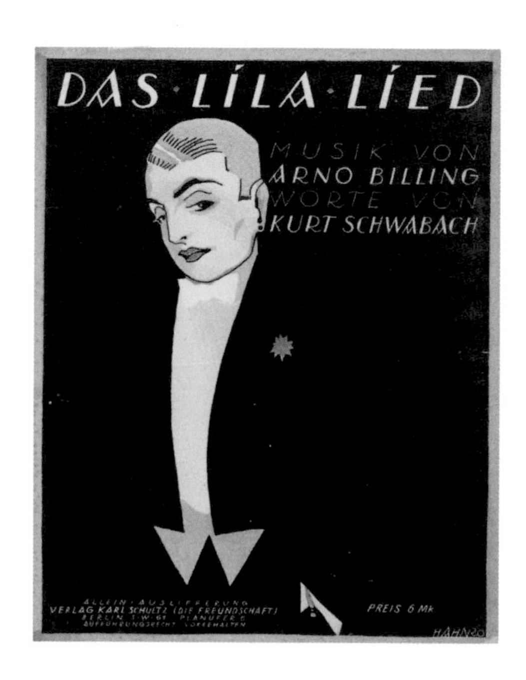

"We're not afraid to be queer and different.
If that means hell—well, hell we'll take the chance.
They're all so straight, uptight, upright and rigid.
They march in lockstep; we prefer to dance.
We see a world of romance and of pleasure.
All they can see is sheer banality.
Lavender nights are our greatest treasure,
where we can be just who we want to be."

—Chorus of "Das Lila Lied" (The Lavender Song)

Left: Marlene Dietrich in a publicity still from the 1930 film *Der Blaue Engel*, which depicts the sexual freedom of Weimar Germany. **Above**: Sheet music of the 1920 German song and gay anthem "Das Lila Lied" (The Lavender Song).

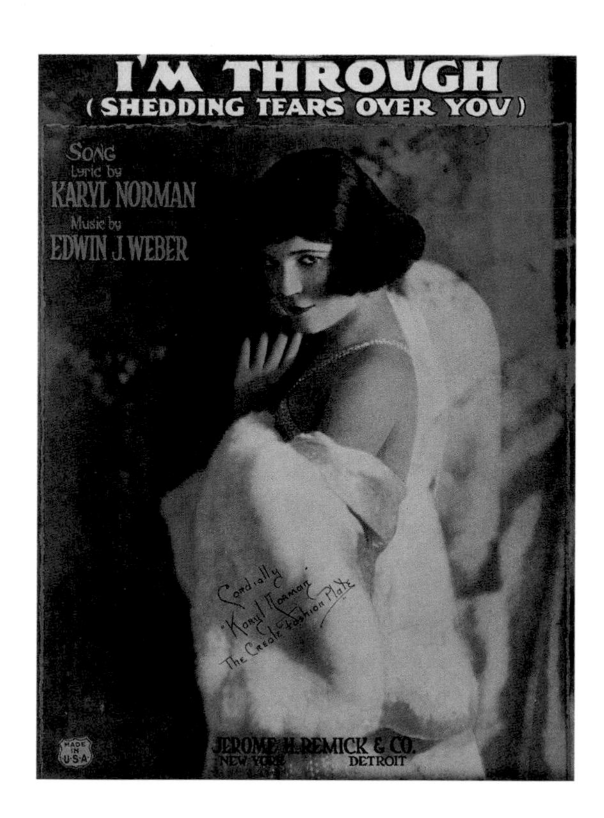

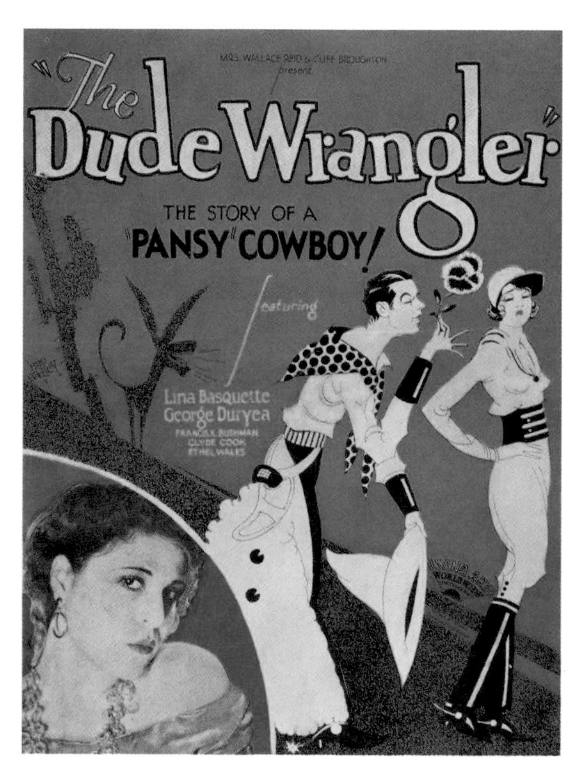

"The release of *The Dude Wrangler* coincided with a peaking phenomenon: possibly the first time since Ancient Greece that homosexuality was truly trendy. The club life in New York City, and a few other places as well, was under the lilac-scented influence of what promptly became known as 'the Pansy Craze.' Gay performers in, partially in, and out of drag became the rage, with such entertainers as Jean Malin and Karyl Norman becoming bona fide celebrities."

—Richard Barrios, *Screened Out: Playing Gay in Hollywood from Edison to Stonewall*, 2003

Opposite: Popular female impersonator Harry S. Franklyn in the 1920s. **Above left**: Sheet music from renowned cross-dresser Karyl Norman, 1922. **Above right**: Movie poster for *The Dude Wrangler: The Story of a "Pansy" Cowboy*, 1930.

GLADYS BENTLEY

Langston Hughes described her as "a large, dark, masculine lady, whose feet pounded the floor while her fingers pounded the keyboard—a perfect piece of African sculpture, animated by her own rhythm." She was the epitome of the Harlem Renaissance.

AMERICAS GREATEST SEPIA PIANA ARTIST
BROWN BOMBER OF SOPHISTICATED SONGS
Gladys Bentley

Downtown New Yorkers were curious in the 1920s—and looking for a drink—so uptown they went to the area of Harlem then known as Jungle Alley, where they found "pansy acts," a sip or two of gin, and Gladys Bentley with short slicked-back hair dressed in white tuxedo, top hat, and tails.

Gladys Alberta Bentley was born in 1907 into a black working-class family in Philadelphia. The oldest of four, she described herself as the problem child, a girl who preferred wearing boys' clothes, a girl who had crushes on her female teachers, a girl who had "strayed from the social norm." So at the age of sixteen she headed for the bright lights of New York City, where she quickly got work entertaining in nightclubs.

She played piano and sang the blues, but she was most admired for her clever, risqué remaking of popular songs. Keeping the tunes, she would add witty and oh-so-dirty lyrics. A critic at the time called her act "one of the rankest revues this commentator has witnessed in many a moon." Nonetheless she was quite popular and very successful, and lived openly as a lesbian, even marrying a woman in 1931.

But as the Great Depression lingered, times turned more conservative, the Harlem Renaissance faded, and Gladys moved to California, often performing at lesbian clubs like Mona's Club 440 in San Francisco.

In 1952—when pressure to conform to the heterosexual norm was at its greatest—she wrote a piece in *Ebony* saying that through the love of a man she had become "a woman again." The marriage did not last, however, and some speculate that this was more survival tactic than truth.

She died in 1960 from complications of the flu.

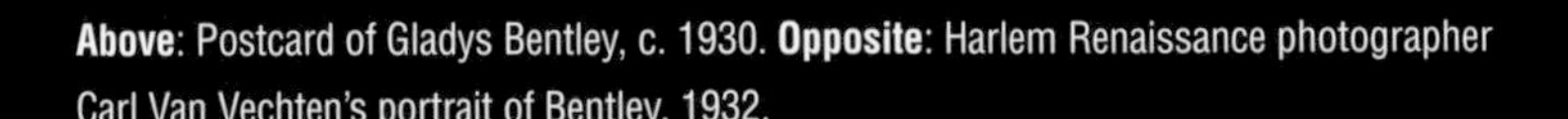

Above: Postcard of Gladys Bentley, c. 1930. **Opposite**: Harlem Renaissance photographer Carl Van Vechten's portrait of Bentley, 1932.

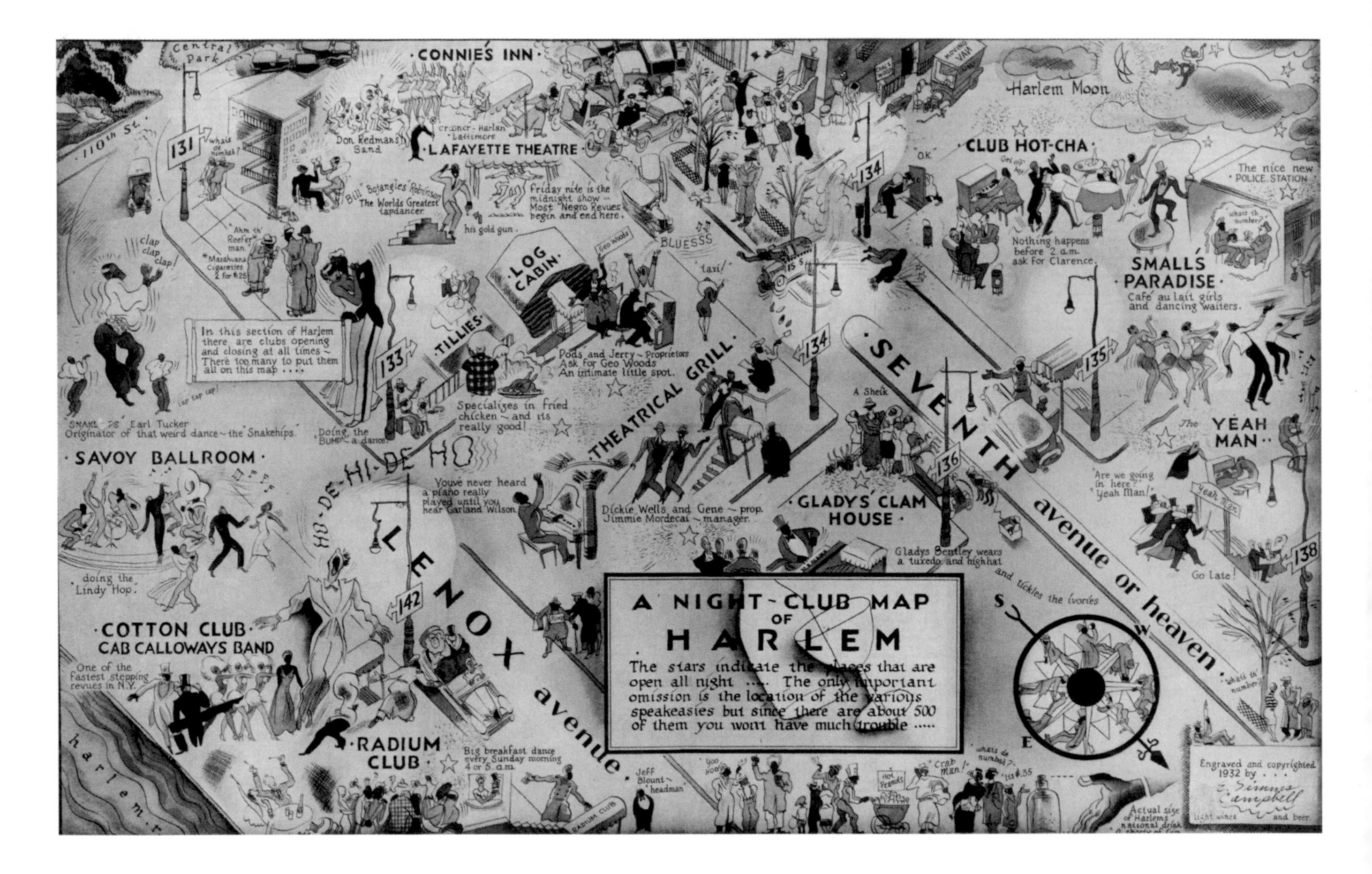

"The Week of a New Yorker: . . . to Romany Marie's, where most of the males don't wear neckties, and most of the females do . . . and to Harlem's Clam House, for specially-built sweet potato pie and to hear Gladys Bentley sing "He's Got Somethin'," which that warbler can . . . "

—*Brooklyn Eagle*, September 23, 1929

Above: Illustrator E. Simms Campbell's 1933 nightclub map of Harlem. See Gladys' Clam House at center right: "Gladys Bentley wears a tuxedo and a high hat and tickles the ivories." **Opposite**: Female impersonators from Mae West's *The Pleasure Man* in front of the Biltmore Theatre are arrested—along with the entire cast—following a police raid at the crowded matinee, October 1, 1928. **Following pages**: *The Fleet's In!* was painted in 1934 by Paul Cadmus while working for the Public Works of Art Project and was originally displayed at the Corcoran Gallery of Art in Washington, DC. It was removed shortly after a retired Navy admiral complained that it was "offensive." Choreographer Jerome Robbins's ballet *Fancy Free* was inspired by the painting.

32

paul cadmu

HOME TIES BROKEN
(World War II)

The onset of World War II sparked a series of changes across society. Where the 1920s gave people a broader taste of humanity (and its sexual possibilities), World War II—in essence a great upheaval—saw more than 16 million Americans (more than 10 percent of the population) joining the armed forces and millions more moving from their small towns to take factory jobs. In essence, people were swept up and then set down in single-sex military barracks around the world and in steel mills, munitions plants, and shipyards in large American cities.

"Everybody was released by the war; people were doing things they hadn't dreamed of in the villages from whence they came."

—Gore Vidal

This was a particularly new world for women, who were not only expected to do their patriotic part by building planes and driving trucks but actually encouraged in this gender role reversal. They were independent, earning money, and often provided with childcare, and they gained a new sense of worth, a new self-esteem. Fanny Christina Hill, an African American woman who worked at a munitions factory, saw it like this: "The war made me live better, it really did. My sister always said that Hitler was the one who got us out of the white folks' kitchen." And for the first time—thanks to Congresswoman Edith Nourse Rogers of Massachusetts, who said, "I was resolved that our women would not again serve with the Army without the same protection the men got"—women served in the armed forces in an official capacity.

But most of all, people were away. Away from their families, away from their hometowns, away from the social constraints and limited thinking that comes with small-town living. At the same time—for both soldiers and newly hired

Opposite: Grinning sailors pose in front of painted palm tree, c. 1942.

factory workers—there was exposure to an array of ideas new to them, everything from pizza to subways to sexual expression.

This sense of freedom and anonymity—often accompanied by a wondrous gay awareness and identity influenced by exposure to world culture—would eventually lead to the formation of gay communities after the war. And because many opted to settle in the cities where they were discharged instead of going back home to live in the closet, there were suddenly large, visible clusters of gay and lesbian folk hanging around town when the war ended.

As Charles Kaiser says in his 1997 book *The Gay Metropolis*, "The combination of friendship and discrimination experienced by homosexuals in uniform created one of the great ironies of gay history: this mixture made the United States Army a secret, powerful, and unwitting engine of gay liberation in America. The roots formed by this experience would nourish the movement that finally made its first public appearance in Manhattan twenty-four years after the war was over." He was talking about Stonewall. But first there was the 1950s to get through.

Above: A c. 1945 snapshot from the private collection of former WAC flight instructor Helen Harder, held at the GLBT Historical Society in San Francisco. **Opposite**: US Navy recruitment poster, illustration by McClelland Barclay, 1942.

Man the GUNS

Join the NAVY

BUT MINE SHALL BE THE FIRST

I found there was a tolerance for lesbianism if they needed you. If you had a job to do that was a specialist kind of a job, or if you were in a theater of operations where bodies were needed, then they tolerated anything, just about. The battalion that I was in was probably about 97 percent lesbian. We were all over the place. And one day I got called in to my commanding general's office, and it happened to be Eisenhower at the time. And he said, "It's come to my attention that there may be some lesbians in the WAC battalion. I'm giving you an order to ferret those lesbians out, and we're going to get rid of them."

I looked at him, and then I looked at his secretary, who was standing next to me, and I said, "Well, sir, if the general pleases, sir, I'll be happy to do this investigation for you. But you have to know that the first name on the list will be mine." He kind of was taken aback a bit. And then this woman standing next to me said, "Sir, if the general pleases, you must be aware that Sergeant Phelps's name may be second, but mine will be first." And then I looked at him and I said, "Sir, you're right, there are lesbians in the WAC battalion. And if the general is prepared to replace all the file clerks, all the section commanders, all of the drivers—every woman in the WAC detachment . . . then I'll be happy to make that list. But I think the general should be aware that among those women are the most highly decorated women in the war. There have been no cases of illegal pregnancies, there have been no cases of AWOL, there have been no cases of misconduct, and as a matter of fact, every six months since we've been here, sir, the general has awarded us a commendation for meritorious service."

And he said, "Forget the order."

—former WAC Sergeant Johnnie Phelps, from the documentary *Before Stonewall: The Making of a Gay and Lesbian Community*, 1984

Above: Nell "Johnnie" Phelps's military headshot, c. 1940. **Opposite**: Recruitment poster for cadet nurses, illustrated by Alex Ross, 1945.

A LIFETIME EDUCATION *FREE*
FOR HIGH SCHOOL GRADUATES WHO QUALIFY

U.S. CADET NURSE CORPS

GO TO YOUR LOCAL HOSPITAL OR WRITE TO U. S. PUBLIC HEALTH SERVICE, BOX 88, NEW YORK 8, N. Y.

INSTALLED 10-2-42
DWG. NO. 6353A-21
A. F. NO. 41-P73200
ANGLE AT 42-27
ANGLE AT 42-00
INDEX 10-90
INSPECTED 10-2-42

"The Women's Army Corps is an integral part of the Army. Not only are there many jobs that women do as efficiently as men, but there are also jobs that women can do better than men."

—Statement from a Women's Army Corps Recruiting Campaign, March 1944

Opposite: A riveting team works on a basic trainer airplane, c. 1942. **Above**: US Women's Army Corps (WAC) nurses in basic training at Camp Blanding, Florida, 1943.

"We have chosen the pink triangle as a symbol. A symbol of the history that others have tried to obliterate, the history that we must recover. And a reminder of where gay oppression can lead if gay people neglect the active struggle for their rights."

—*The Body Politic*, Canadian gay liberation journal, 1971–1987

Above: Prisoners at the Sachsenhausen concentration camp in Oranienburg, Germany, wearing pink triangles identifying them as gay, December 19, 1938. Nazi law only dealt with "unnatural sexual offences between men," so lesbians were usually spared. Other triangles seen at the camps: political prisoners wore red, career criminals wore green, "asocials" wore black, Jehovah's Witnesses wore purple, Roma and Sinti wore brown, and those who attempted to flee the country but were caught wore blue. Jews wore a yellow star.
Opposite: A World War II–era Nazi concentration camp uniform for homosexuals.

48841

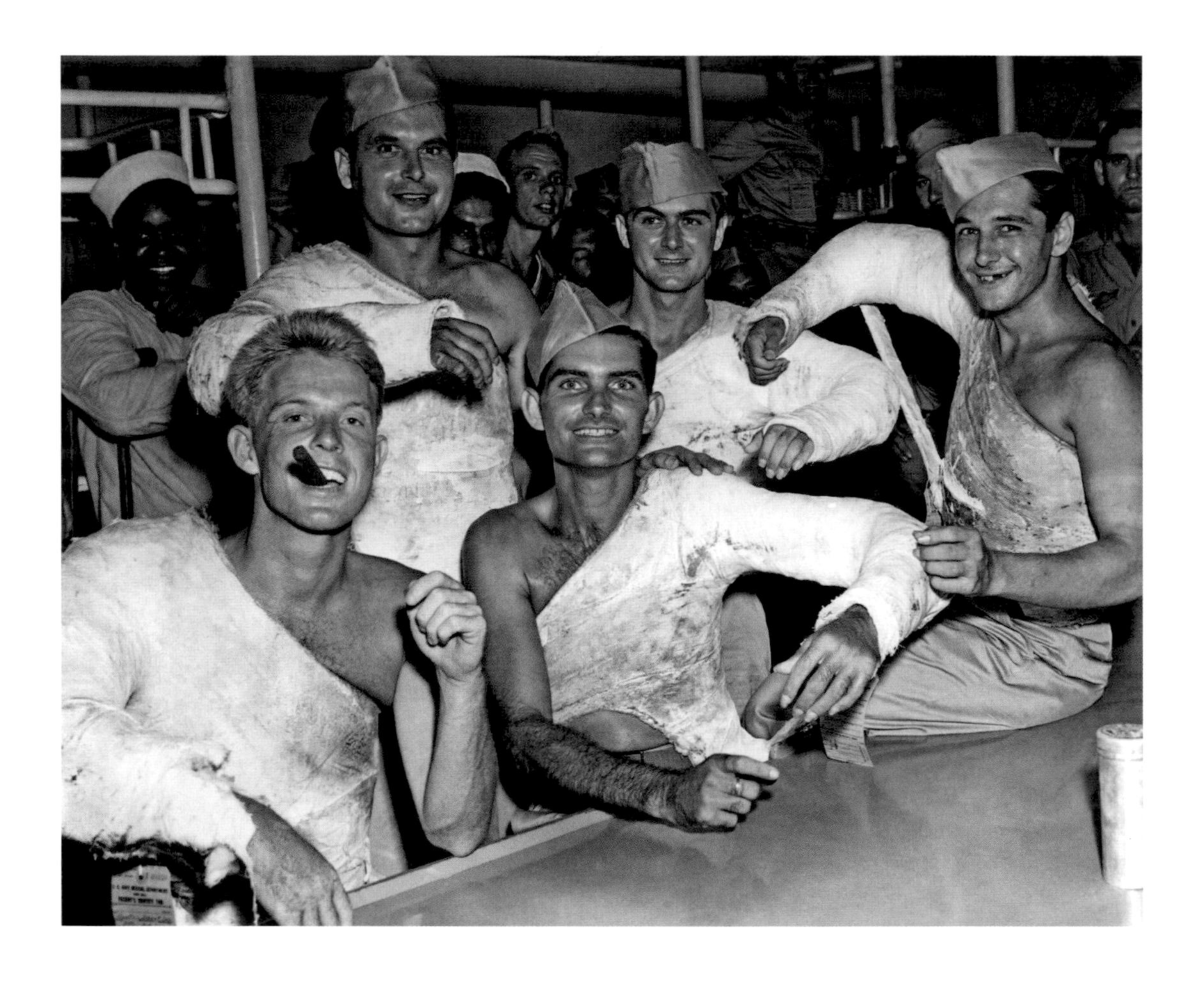

"Men on battleships and battlefields lived together in close quarters with little privacy. . . . Servicemen in these all-male groups turned to their fellow troops for emotional and psychological support. The stress of leaving home, shipping out, active battle, and years of war allowed men to be vulnerable with one another in ways impossible outside of this environment."

—Michael Bronski, political organizer, writer, and editor, in *A Queer History of the United States*, 2011

Above: US veterans arrive home, New York City, August 14, 1945. **Opposite**: Detail from a World War II "Buy War Bonds" poster illustrated by Joseph Hirsch, 1942.

TILL WE MEET AGAIN

MATTACHINE SOCIETY, INC.
OF NEW YORK
E.C.H.O.
(EAST COAST HOMOPHILE ORGANIZATION
OFFICE HOURS
MON. THRU FRI. 6-9 P.M.
SATURDAY 2-5 P.M.
OTHER HOURS BY APPOINTMENT
IF NOT IN, INQUIRE
ROOM 221 or
CALL: WA 4-774

BACK IN THE CLOSET
(The 1950s)

After the war there was a brief but important period of postwar gay-culture awareness and elation as soldiers settled in the city where they were discharged instead of heading back to the farm. "We're Here" happened during the war while "We're Queer" was bubbling along in the background. There were popular books like 1948's *The City and the Pillar*, a gay coming-of-age story by Gore Vidal, and *Giovanni's Room*, James Baldwin's 1956 story of David, an American in Paris exploring his sexuality with the help of an Italian bartender. William S. Burroughs, Jack Kerouac, and Allen Ginsberg all wrote about homosexuality or bisexuality, and Burroughs and Ginsberg lived openly. And though the plot—equal parts tragedy and porn—often went badly for the main characters in the era's pulp fiction, this genre was a major source of lesbian love, what historian Joan Nestle called the "survival literature" of lesbians in the 1950s.

"I knew the government was going to look for a new enemy . . . [and that] would be us, the queers. . . . the one group of disenfranchised people who did not even know they were a group. . . . We had to get started. It was high time. "

—Harry Hay, Mattachine Society founder

And then there was Alfred Kinsey and his book *Sexual Behavior in the Human Male* (1948). Only five thousand copies were printed, and it was anything but sexy, but it sure made a splash. "At least 37 percent of the male population has some homosexual experience," it said, and it backed that up with science and, more importantly, no moral judgment. Kinsey continued, "In view of the data . . . it is difficult to maintain the view that psychosexual reactions between individuals of the same sex are rare and therefore abnormal or unnatural."

Opposite: Dick Leitsch, Mattachine Society of New York president from 1965 to 1969, at the Society's office in December 1965.

But mostly, there was repression. Conformity ruled the day. "We knew we were outside the pale," writer, womanist, and civil rights activist Audre Lorde stated in Charles Kaiser's 1997 book *The Gay Metropolis*. "We were dykes. A lot of us were artists. We hated typing. We didn't want straight jobs. We were the fringe. And that was because of the fifties."

The Lavender Scare followed the Red Scare as Senator Joseph McCarthy (and his closeted comrade Roy Cohn) tried to rid the federal government of gay and lesbian employees. Secretary of Commerce Charles Sawyer wrote to the investigation committee, "The privilege of working for the United States Government should not be extended to persons of dubious moral character, such as homosexuals or sex perverts." At the movies, any hint of queerness was dealt with as salacious or criminal or buffoonery and, as Mikayla Mislak said in an April 2015 issue of *Filmic Magazine*, "The characters were . . . never depicted with any tangible humanity." And TV was just plain sexless.

Still, the civil rights movements began to stir as returning black servicemen and women—1.2 million of them—faced bigotry and prejudice, the opposite of what they'd fought for. Women, too, had seen new possibilities. During the war they were soldiers and breadwinners. They realized they could be as competent, as free, as in-charge as men, and the world didn't end, nor did society collapse.

In these newly forming and newly visible conclaves of gayness in cities around the country, people began to organize and to even fight back.

In 1950, Harry Hay (and six other brave souls) formed the Mattachine Society to "educate homosexuals and heterosexuals toward an ethical homosexual culture paralleling the cultures of the Negro, Mexican and Jewish peoples" and to "assist gays who are victimized daily as a result of oppression."

Shortly thereafter, Del Martin and Phyllis Lyon, a couple since 1952, helped form the Daughters of Bilitis. At first they were just looking for friends, other lesbians to hang out with. But soon their social club became "a woman's organization for the purpose of promoting the integration of the homosexual into society."

And in 1957, Frank Kameny, a Harvard-educated astronomer who was fired from the Army Map Service for being gay, got mad and took his fight to the Supreme Court.

Times they were a-changin'.

Above: Book cover of *Queer Affair* by Carol Emery, c. 1957. **Opposite**: Idealized image of 1950s family life.

CHRISTINE JORGENSEN

Reflecting on her impact in post–World War II America, the country's first transgender celebrity declared, "We didn't start the sexual revolution, but I think we gave it a good kick in the pants!"

Bronx-born Christine Jorgensen's glamorous transformation in the early 1950s introduced the American public to transsexuality. Blonde, attractive, and genteel, Christine fit neatly into the Cold War–era feminine ideal and became a sensation overnight when the *New York Daily News* broke her story on December 1, 1952. The front-page headline—the first of many—blared: EX-GI BECOMES BLONDE BEAUTY.

She grew up as a self-described shy, frail, introverted child in a Danish-American family, served a two-year stint in the Army as a clerk, and started a career in photography before seeking scientific help to understand why she was miserable in her male body. After an endocrinologist explained that her high estrogen levels made her "a woman trapped in a man's body," she spent two years in Copenhagen to undergo a medical transition. She named herself Christine in honor of her surgeon, Danish hormone expert Dr. Christian Hamburger. "Nature made the mistake which I have had corrected," she explained to her parents in a letter, "and now I am your daughter."

"If you understand trans-genders then you understand that gender doesn't have to do with bed partners, it has to do with identity."

—Christine Jorgensen

At age twenty-six, Christine Jorgensen arrived home in New York, stepping off the plane in a fur coat and hat and, according to the Hearst newswire, "well-filled nylon stockings" to a throng of three hundred reporters and photographers. She launched a career on the television talk show circuit, spoke frequently on college campuses, performed in her own nightclub act, and wrote an autobiography that inspired the 1970 film *The Christine Jorgensen Story*. In 1989, after a long battle with bladder and lung cancer, Jorgensen died at age sixty-two. Her outspoken views on the fluidity of gender resonated with young audiences headed into the sexual revolution of the 1960s—and still inspire today.

ICON

Opposite: Christine Jorgensen aboard the SS *United States*, August 7, 1954.

"And these nights were being acted out under a foreign sky, with no-one to watch, no penalties attached–it was this last fact which was our undoing, for nothing is more unbearable, once one has it, than freedom." —James Baldwin, from *Giovanni's Room*, 1956

Above: Writer William S. Burroughs (left), journalist Lucien Carr (center), and poet Allen Ginsberg (right) in New York City, c. 1957.
Opposite: James Baldwin posing for gay photographer (and Harlem Renaissance chronicler) Carl Van Vechten, 1955.

HARRY HAY

"We are an oppressed cultural minority." With that statement, social activist and self-schooled Marxist Harry Hay pioneered the idea that homosexuals are discriminated against in the same way as racial minorities. Original, brilliant, controversial, and visionary, Hay set the stage for the gay rights movement in the 1950s and 1960s and launched one of the first national gay rights organizations, the Mattachine Society.

The society's "Missions and Purposes" statement, written by Hay and a small group of cofounders in 1951, has been called "one of the seminal declarations of Queer liberation." The document seeks to inform and enlighten the public about homosexuality and empower homosexuals to feel that they have a "dignified and useful role to play in society."

As a young man in the 1930s, Hay felt compelled to hide his homosexuality (it was illegal, after all), and as an active member of the gay-rejecting Communist Party he got married and adopted two daughters. Family man by day and secret homosexual by night, he remained in his marriage for more than a decade until his wife, Anita Platky, asked for a divorce. She knew he was gay, but once his affiliation with the Mattachine Society went public, she feared their children would be ostracized. At about the same time, Hay disconnected himself from the Communist Party and freed himself of its hostile stance on homosexuality.

In 1955, Hay became a target of Senator Joseph McCarthy's House Un-American Activities Committee. Years after being acquitted of all allegations during what he called "the terror of the McCarthy anti-homosexual inquisitions," he cofounded the Gay Liberation Front chapter in Los Angeles. In 1979, as a rejection of the gay community's assimilation into commercialized mainstream society, Hay cofounded the counterculture Radical Faeries. Since the first Spiritual Gathering of Radical Faeries, the movement has become a global network of "sanctuaries" from mainstream queer culture. Hay passed away in 2002, leaving a powerful legacy of steering the first advances toward LGBTQ+ rights.

ICON

Above: Publicity still of Harry Hay performing as an openly gay character in the Clifford Odets play *Till the Day I Die*, May 1935. **Opposite**: Robert Giard portrait of Harry Hay, 1989.

Opposite: Wisconsin senator Joseph McCarthy (left) and his aide (the closeted) Roy Cohn during the House Un-American Activities Committee investigations, 1954. **Above**: Activist Frank Kameny (second in line) with a group of "homosexual American citizens" picketing outside the White House on Armed Forces Day, May 21, 1955. The protestors sought "to end the issuance of less-than-fully honorable discharges to homosexuals in the Armed Forces, to allow homosexuals in the Armed Forces, and to meet with the Departments of Defense, Army, Navy, and Air Force to engage constructive discussion of the policies and procedures at issue."

DEL MARTIN AND PHYLLIS LYON

In 1955, Del Martin and Phyllis Lyon—living together since Valentine's Day 1953—were among the first members of a secret lesbian club in San Francisco that eventually became the Daughters of Bilitis (DOB; from the poem by Pierre Louÿs), the first national lesbian civil rights and political organization in the United States. Members met in each other's homes to dance, have a drink, and avoid the police raids that regularly rained down on gay and lesbian bars. The Daughters offered a haven for lesbians who sought community in an era when they were "isolated and separated—and scared," said Lyon.

"The Daughters began in a climate of fear, rejection, and oppression, the aftermath of Congressional hearings and witch hunts by Wisconsin senator Joseph McCarthy, who was relentless in 'exposing' Communists and homosexuals in government," Lyon wrote in a 1995 article in the *Gay & Lesbian Review*.

Lyon and Martin organized public forums in which lawyers educated the audience about the law and civil rights, and psychologists refuted the "sickness theory" of homosexuality and "promoted self-acceptance," according to Lyon. "From the beginning," she said, "DOB was engaged in peer counseling and internal discussion groups to allay fears and build self-esteem."

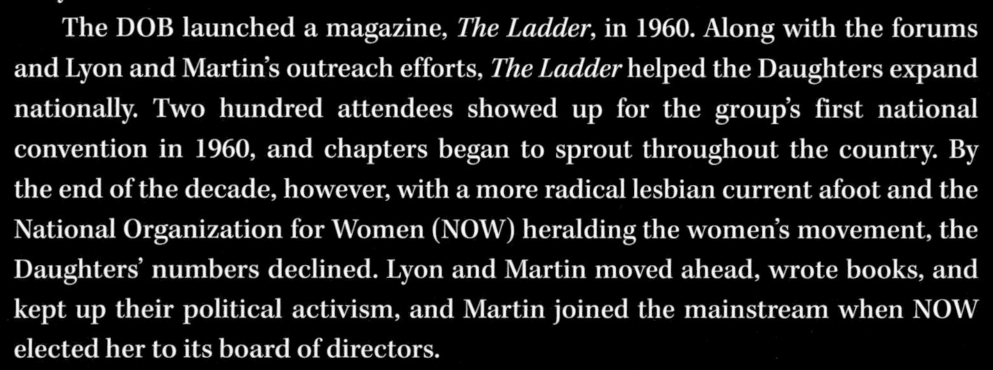

The DOB launched a magazine, *The Ladder*, in 1960. Along with the forums and Lyon and Martin's outreach efforts, *The Ladder* helped the Daughters expand nationally. Two hundred attendees showed up for the group's first national convention in 1960, and chapters began to sprout throughout the country. By the end of the decade, however, with a more radical lesbian current afoot and the National Organization for Women (NOW) heralding the women's movement, the Daughters' numbers declined. Lyon and Martin moved ahead, wrote books, and kept up their political activism, and Martin joined the mainstream when NOW elected her to its board of directors.

Lyon and Martin were the first couple married in San Francisco when same-sex marriage became legal in 2008. They had already been together for fifty-five years, but Martin's death from a fall just weeks later was a tragic end to a legendary relationship that had helped reshape society.

Opposite: Robert Giard portrait of Del Martin (left) and Phyllis Lyon, 1989. **Above**: *The Ladder*, October 1957.

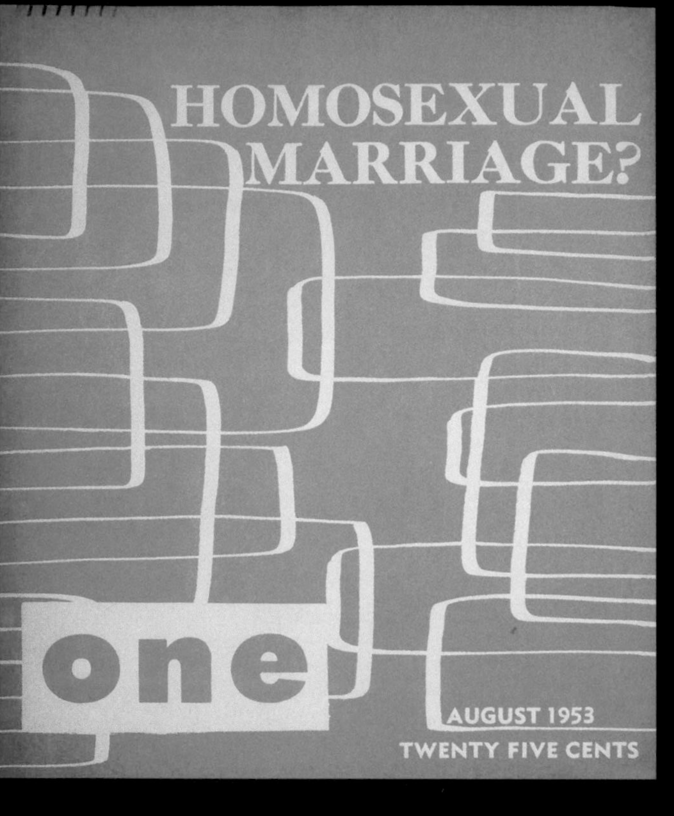
HOMOSEXUAL
MARRIAGE?
one
AUGUST 1953
TWENTY FIVE CENTS

one
THE HOMOSEXUAL VIEWPOINT
What about Gay Bars?
one
The
Homosexual
Magazine
..are
"normals"
abnormally
interested
in
sex?
NOVEMBER 1953
TWENTY-FIVE CENTS

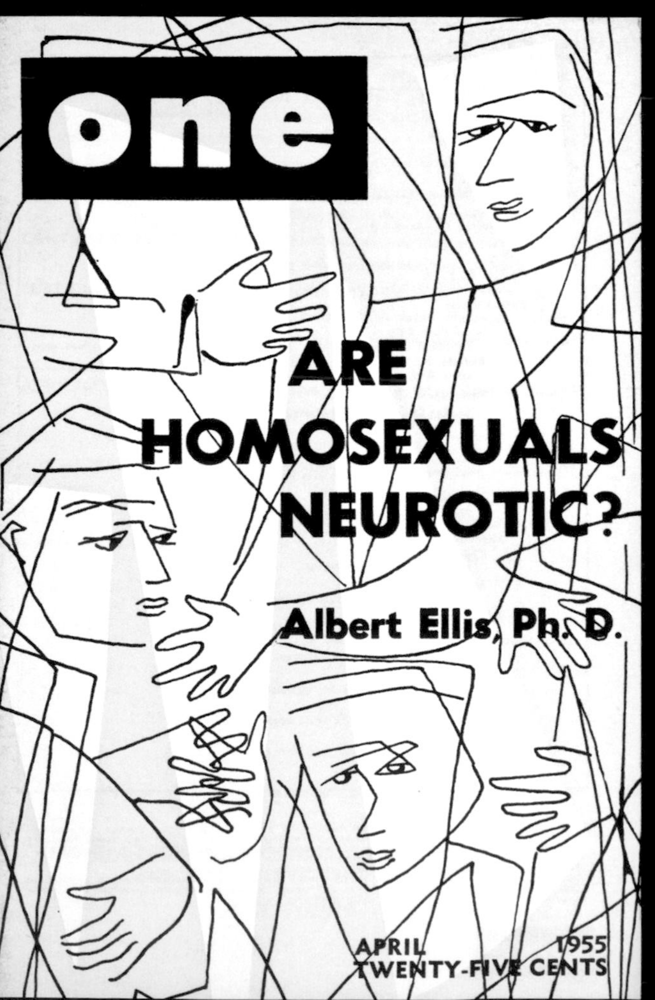
one
ARE
HOMOSEXUALS
NEUROTIC?
Albert Ellis, Ph. D.
APRIL 1955
TWENTY-FIVE CENTS

"... WITHOUT ALTERING SOCIETY ITSELF"

In every sphere, religious, economic, political, our life is composed of a mass of little engagements in which those of like viewpoint group together, and defend themselves against those of contrary viewpoint, and fight it out, usually inconclusively. This condition of engagement never ends, regardless of the momentary outcome, because it is a basic ingredient of life.

The important thing here is not the result of the engagement so much as the satisfaction, the feeling of belonging socially, of partaking in life, of being accepted by life, the happiness that is the result of the joining together with persons of like viewpoint. That is what human life boils down to, I think.

The fight never ends. It sometimes succeeds in its objectives or approaches closer to it and of course thereby adds more to human happiness, but the important thing is not the outcome of the engagement but the successful grouping for the engagement. Before happiness can be derived from the distant victory, very real satisfaction and happiness can be extracted from the very necessary grouping for the engagement, and in many cases the only real result can be the happiness resulting from belonging to this articulate group.

—J.B.S., anonymous essayist from *One*, August 1953

Opposite: Covers of *One,* the first American pro-gay political magazine.

GAY PRIDE

PART 2
WE'RE QUEER . . .

ROAD TO REBELLION
(The 1960s)

One spring night in 1959, two of LAPD's finest entered Cooper Do-nuts, a hangout on Main Street in what was then the gay and seedy part of Los Angeles. The shop was popular with the trans community (because they were allowed in). The police were there to harass and arrest as usual, but as a group of arrested patrons were being put into the squad car, the customers inside the shop rebelled, and suddenly people were—according to *The Gay Revolution* author Lillian Faderman—"turning donuts into flying missiles, flinging cups, sugar cubes, anything hurlable lobbing them at the heads of the offending officers."

> **"We as liberated homosexual activists demand the freedom for expression of our dignity and value as human beings."**
>
> —Arthur Evans, Gay Activists Alliance Statement of Purpose

Six years later, on the other side of the country, gay men and lesbians from Philadelphia, New York, and Washington, DC, got together for the first Annual Reminder protest. In their perfectly pressed dresses and their respectable jackets and ties (all gender appropriate), they peacefully picketed in front of Independence Hall in Philadelphia. The goal: to remind America that a large group of its citizens was being denied their rights. "Without our demonstrations starting in '65, Stonewall would not have happened," recalled Frank Kameny, who, along with Barbara Gittings, was a main organizer.

The following summer, late into the night at Gene Compton's twenty-four-hour cafeteria in San Francisco's Tenderloin neighborhood, the police came in to (as usual) harass and arrest. But one of the drag queens had had enough, and when an officer grabbed her, she threw coffee in his face. Suddenly sugar shakers

Previous pages: The first anniversary Stonewall march, then known as Gay Liberation Day (and later Gay Pride Day) on Sixth Avenue at Milligan Place, New York, June 28, 1970. **Opposite**: Early gay rights activist, author, and cofounder of the Gay Activists Alliance (GAA) Arthur Evans protesting anti-gay employment practices at the Fidelifacts employment agency, 1971.

were airborne and windows were breaking. In the street, drag queens resisted arrest, a cop car was trashed, and a newsstand was set afire. The oppressed came back the next night, along with their supporters, to protest. "We got tired of being harassed. We got tired of being made to go into the men's room when we were dressed like women. We wanted our rights," Amanda St. Jaymes, a transgender woman, commented in the 2005 documentary *Screaming Queens*.

Much less violent—though maybe not as satisfying as throwing a sugar shaker through a plate glass window—was the 1966 "Sip-In" at Julius' in Greenwich Village, which turned into a kind of pub crawl with a purpose. Three members of the Mattachine Society set out to challenge the State Liquor Authority's regulation denying service to homosexuals. Though it took a few tries—at the Waikiki bar the manager asked, "How do I know you're homosexuals?" and gave them drinks on the house—they were eventually denied service at Julius' (newspaper reporters in tow) and took their case to court. In the end, the court ruled that homosexuals could not be prevented from peacefully assembling or from being served alcohol.

On New Year's Eve 1967, at the Black Cat Bar on Sunset Boulevard in Los Angeles, undercover cops waited for the countdown. "Two males kissing each other was against the law," activist Alexei Romanoff explained in a 2017 NPR interview. As the clock struck twelve, the police pounced and more than a dozen people were arrested. Two had to register as sex offenders—for sharing a New Year's kiss. Romanoff's reaction: "Absolute anger. Once again, we're being picked on." Five weeks later, a group called Personal Rights in Defense and Education (PRIDE) organized over five hundred people to protest.

"There was no going back now. We had discovered a power that we weren't even aware that we had."

—Danny Garvin, Stonewall demonstrator

And then there was Stonewall. On a hot summer night in a small bar on Christopher Street in Greenwich Village about two hundred of its usual patrons—a mix of street kids, gay, lesbian, and trans people—were drinking and dancing. Officer Seymour Pine, then commander of lower Manhattan's vice squad, and about half a dozen or so of his men, came to the Stonewall Inn to raid it. But things didn't go according to plan, and for the next five nights angry mobs protested in and around the bar. (See pages 71–73.)

"The Stonewall uprising is the signal event in American gay and lesbian civil rights history because it transformed a small movement that existed prior to that night into a mass movement," David Carter, author of *Stonewall: The Riots That Sparked the Gay Revolution*, said in an interview. "It is to the gay movement what the fall of the Bastille is to the unleashing of the French Revolution."

Opposite: The first issue of *Gay Power*, a local newspaper covering the culture and politics of New York's gay scene, 1969.

VOLUME 1 #1

PRICE 35¢

Out Of Town 75¢

JUST A DROP
HELPS KEEP

VISIT THE

THREE ARTICLES OF CLOTHING

WILLIAM ESKRIDGE (professor of law): In states like New York, there were a whole basket of crimes that gay people could be charged with. One was the 1845 statute that made it a crime in the state to masquerade.

FRED SARGEANT: Three articles of clothing had to be of your gender or you would be in violation of that law.

MARTIN BOYCE: Mind you, socks didn't count, so it was underwear, and undershirt, now the next thing was going to ruin the outfit.

—from the 2011 PBS American Experience documentary *Stonewall Uprising*

Previous pages: Trans sex workers in New York City's Times Square, 1965. **Above** and **Opposite**: Forty-four men were arrested on charges of "impersonation" and "indecent exposure" while attending the National Variety Artists' Exotic Carnival and Ball at the Manhattan Center, October 26, 1962.

3 DEVIATES INVITE EXCLUSION BY BARS

Mr. Leitsch and two other [Mattachine] society officials, Craig Rodwell, 25 years old, and John Timmons, 21, had planned their noon-time sip-in at the Ukrainian-American Village Restaurant, 12 St. Marks Place, in East Greenwich Village, because the establishment displays a sign reading: "If You Are Gay, Please Go Away." But the restaurant was closed.

At Howard Johnson's Restaurant at Avenue of the Americas and Eighth Street, Mr. Leitsch read a statement identifying the group as homosexuals and asked for service. The manager, Emile Varela, 55, doubled with laughter and had a waiter bring three bourbons to them. He said he knew of no regulation against serving homosexuals and that if it existed he did not agree with it. "I drink," Mr. Varela said, "and who's to say whether I'm a homosexual or not."

The three homosexuals again were served with drinks in The Waikiki, 132 Avenue of the Americas, a block away.

From the Waikiki, the testing team walked two more blocks to Julius's.

Jack, the manager there, said he had to refuse service after Mr. Leitsch identified the group as homosexuals. "I think it's in the law," the manager said.

—*The New York Times*, Friday, April 22, 1966

Opposite: Mattachine Society members, from left, John Timmins (with coat on shoulder), Dick Leitsch (facing bartender), Craig Rodwell, and Randy Wicker stage a sip-in at Julius' Bar, April 1966.

WE HOMOSEXUALS PLEAD WITH
OUR PEOPLE TO PLEASE HELP
MAINTAIN PEACEFUL AND QUIET
CONDUCT ON THE STREETS OF
THE VILLAGE - MATTACHINE

Left: Outside the Stonewall Inn on Christopher Street in Greenwich Village, June 28, 1969.
Above: A hand-painted sign by the Mattachine Society on the boarded-up window of the Stonewall Inn during the riots, June 1969.

A REPORT FROM THE FRONT

by Edmund White, from *The Gay & Lesbian Review*, Summer 1994

I wrote this letter to Alfred Corn, who would go on to become one of the leading poets of my generation, and to Amy Jones, at that time his wife (she would become an important Renaissance scholar in comparative literature). Alfred and Ann were among my closest friends. They had been living in Paris for a year when I wrote them. Aflred was quite open about being bisexual, so I knew my letter would fall on friendly ears. The letter is not entirely accurate and the tone is rather frivolous—signs of how lightly even the participants took an event they had no idea would become historic. Stonewall took a while to transform us all; I wrote this letter to entertain before the transformation had taken place.

July 8, 1969

Dear Ann and Alfred,

Well the big news here is Gay Power. It's the most extraordinary thing. It all began two weeks ago on a Friday night. The cops raided the Stonewall, that mighty Bastille which you know has remained impregnable for three years, so brazen and so conspicuous that one could only surmise that the Mafia was paying off the pigs handsomely. Apparently, however, a new police official, Sergeant Smith, has taken over the Village, and he's a peculiarly diligent lawman. In any event, a mammoth paddy wagon, as big as a school bus, pulled up to the Wall and about ten cops raided the joint. The kids were all shooed into the street; soon other gay kids and straight spectators swelled the ranks to, I'd say, about a thousand people. Christopher Street was completely blocked off and the crowds swarmed from the *Voice* office down to the Civil War hospital.

As the Mafia owners were dragged out one by one and shoved into the wagon, the crowd would let out Bronx cheers and jeers and clapping. Someone shouted "Gay Power," others took up the cry—and then it dissolved into giggles. A few more prisoners—bartenders, hatcheck boys—a few more cheers, someone starts singing "We Shall Overcome"—and they started camping on it. A drag queen is shoved into

Opposite: A group of street kids celebrate outside the boarded-up Stonewall Inn, June 1969.

the wagon; she hits the cop over the head with her purse. The cop clubs her. Angry stirring in the crowd. The cops, used to the cringing and the disorganization of the gay crowd, snort off. But the crowd doesn't disperse. Everyone is restless, angry, and high-spirited. No one has a slogan, no one even has an attitude, but something's brewing.

Some adorable butch hustler boy pulls up a *parking meter*, mind you, out of the pavement, and uses it as a battering ram (a few cops are still inside the Wall, locked in). The boys begin to pound at the heavy wooden double doors and windows; glass shatters all over the street. Cries of "Liberate the Bar." Bottles (from hostile straights?) rain down from the apartment windows. Cries of "We're the Pink Panthers." A Negro queen whirls like a dervish with a twisted piece of metal in her hand and breaks the remaining windows. The door begins to give. The cops turn a hose on the crowd (they're still within the Wall). But they can't aim it properly, and the crowd sticks. Finally the door is broken down and the kids, as though working to a prior plan, systematically dump refuse from the waste cans into the Wall, squirting it with lighter fluid, and ignite it. Huge flashes of flame and billows of smoke.

Now the cops in the paddy wagon return, and the two fire engines pull up. Clubs fly. The crowd retreats.

Saturday night, the pink panthers are back in full force. The cops form a flying wedge at the Greenwich Avenue end of Christopher and drive the kids down towards Sheridan Square. The panthers, however, run down Waverly, up Gay Street, and come out *behind* the cops, kicking in a chorus line, taunting, screaming. Dreary middle-class East Side queens stand around disapproving but fascinated, unable to go home, as though torn between their class loyalties, their desire to be respectable, and their longing for freedom. Sheridan Square is cordoned off by the cops. The United Cigar store closes, Riker's closes, the deli closes. No one can pass through the square; to walk up Seventh Avenue, you must detour all the way to Bleecker.

A mad left-wing group of straight kids called the Crazies is trying to organize the gay kids, pointing out that Lindsay is to blame (the Crazies want us to vote for Procaccino, or "Prosciutto," as we call him). A Crazy girl launches into a tirade against Governor Rockefeller, "whose empire," she cries, "must be destroyed." Straight Negro boys put their arms around me and say we're comrades (it's okay with me—in fact, great, the first camaraderie I've felt with blacks in years). Mattachine (our NAACP) hands out leaflets about "what to do if arrested." Some man from the Oscar Wilde bookstore hands out a leaflet describing to newcomers what's going on. I give a stump speech about the need to radicalize, how we must recognize we're part of a

The boys begin to pound at the heavy wooden double doors and windows; glass shatters all over the street. Cries of "Liberate the Bar."

vast rebellion of all the repressed. Some jeers, some cheers. Charles Burch plans to make a plastique to hurl at cops.

Sunday night, the Stonewall, now reopened—though one room is charred and blasted, all lights are smashed, and only a few dim bulbs are burning, no hard liquor being sold—the management posts an announcement: "We appreciate all of you and your efforts to help, but the Stonewall believes in peace. Please end the riots. We believe in peace." Some kids, nonetheless, try to turn over a cop car. Twelve are arrested. Some straight toughs rough up some queens. The queens beat them up. Sheridan Square is again blocked off by the pigs. That same night a group of about seventy-five vigilantes in Queens chop down a wooded part of a park as vengeance against the perverts who are cruising in the bushes. "They're endangering our women and children." The *Times*, which has scarcely mentioned the Sheridan Square riots (a half column, very tame), is now so aroused by the *conservation* issue that it blasts the "vigs" for their malice toward *nature*.

Wednesday. The *Voice* runs two front-page stories on the riots, both snide, both devoted primarily to assuring readers that the authors are straight.

The last weekend, nothing much happens because it was the Fourth of July and everyone was away. Charles Burch has decided it's all a drag. When he hears that gay kids are picketing Independence Hall in Philly because they're being denied their constitutional rights, he says: "But of course, the Founding Fathers didn't intend to protect *perverts* and *criminals*." Who knows what will happen this weekend, or this week? I'll keep you posted.

I miss you both frightfully. No more fun dinners, no endless telephone conversations, no sharing of exquisite sensation, gad it's awful.

Love, Ed

EDMUND WHITE is an American novelist, memoirist, and an essayist on literary and social topics. Much of his writing—including A Boy's Own Story, The Beautiful Room is Empty, *and* The Joy of Gay Sex—*is on the theme of same-sex love.*

MART CROWLEY
THE BOYS IN
THE BAND
L+D Dillon

STONEWALL AS EVENT AND IDEA

by Michael Denneny, from *The Gay & Lesbian Review*, Summer 1994

As we celebrate the twenty-fifth anniversary of the Stonewall riots, much is being written about that now mythical event which is generally taken as the birth of the contemporary gay and lesbian rights movement. Much of what I have read strikes me as wrong-headed, especially the revisionist attempts by the currently politically correct to downplay the role of white males in that event. "Middle-class white men" is the term generally used, but considering the reputation of the Stonewall, or just glancing at the few photos left from that time and place, one wonders about the term "middle class"; one wonders about the word "men." "Randy white boys" might be more accurate. Recently I read a manuscript proposal (generated by a PBS television series on gay rights) that asserted that "middle-class white men" had "stolen" (their word) Stonewall as an event, appropriating to themselves an action generated by lesbians, transvestites, and people of color. The authors offered no evidence for this statement, just blandly asserting this revision of history with the same smug and self-righteous certainty that Stalin's encyclopedists must have felt as they dutifully revised their history decade after decade.

Personally, I doubt that the Stonewall, while clearly a racially mixed bar, was ever a popular dyke hangout, or that its clientele was anything like equally divided between men and women. And while anyone who knew Marsha or Sylvia knew what a force Street Transvestite Action Revolutionaries (their term) could be in a confrontation with the cops, the contribution of either to the ongoing organizing of the gay movement is a different question.

But, in retrospect, all these squabbles to claim credit are not only petty but beside the point, except when they interfere with the attempt to ascertain

Opposite: Book cover for Mart Crowley's controversial play *The Boys in the Band*, illustrated by Leo and Diane Dillon, 1968.

What was decisive was not the event itself, but how people responded, the immediate, spontaneous, and utterly decentralized flurry of organizing, leafleting, and pamphleteering that resulted.

historically what actually happened. They are beside the point because they misunderstand how an event like Stonewall actually comes to interact with history, becomes a part of history, or not. Stonewall was not the first time gay people had confronted the police, nor the first time we stood up for ourselves. John Preston once told me about a gay bar in Chicago a year or so earlier. The police were harassing the owners and made the patrons walk a long gauntlet of cops while being photographed entering and leaving the place. For the people involved, this confrontation was as harrowing and as heroic as Stonewall, but it had no echo across the country and is now almost forgotten. There had also been a similar confrontation in LA.

So what made Stonewall different?

Kant wrote of the French Revolution that it was not so much the rioting that was going to change the world as the quality of attention paid to it by spectators, by those observers across Europe who watched the unfolding events in Paris and came to believe that something momentous had happened. It was what the spectators made of the events of the French Revolution that would change history, not what the rioters in Paris had done. In other words, it is when an event is raised to the level of an idea that it has the power to alter history through the consciousness of people.

I would argue that something similar is the case with Stonewall. It was definitely not the first sign of the emerging gay revolt. A year and a half before Stonewall, a couple of guys had started *The Advocate* in Los Angeles, at about the same time that Troy Perry had established the first of the Metropolitan Community Churches, today the largest gay organization in the world. Clearly, something was afoot with gay people even before the events at Stonewall. What was missing was any sense of possibility, any alternative, to the oppression gay people faced daily everywhere they looked.

To get a sense of the mental oppression our people labored under, this lack of possibility that was so spiritually suffocating, one might look at Mart Crowley's play *The Boys in the Band*, a much maligned work that precisely delineates the pre-revolutionary emotional situation that would lead to Stonewall. The play is about eight gay men and one straight; in essence, the gay guys, who are very unhappy and bitchy, start the evening beating up on each other and progress till their anger is directed at the straight man. What is amazing in this play is that none of the gay characters has any sense of possibility, any way out of the trap of gay life as it was then led. Although they are clearly angry to the point of fury, the idea of gay liberation is the furthest thing from their minds. As someone who remembers the years before Stonewall, I can testify that the very concept of gay liberation would have then struck most of us, even those of us who were intensely politically active, as absurd. Being homosexual was a psychological situation, maybe a medical situation, but certainly not a political matter.

Luckily for everyone, the women's movement came along and got us to consider the notion that the personal *was* political: a major step forward. Then what was needed was a crystallizing moment, and the five continuous nights of rioting that the raid on Stonewall provoked offered that moment. What was decisive was not the event itself, but how people responded, the immediate, spontaneous, and utterly decentralized flurry of organizing, leafleting, and pamphleteering that resulted (and which was so well documented in Donn Teal's 1972 book *The Gay Militants*). It was this response, and perhaps above all the late Craig Rodwell's determination to commemorate the event the next June with the world's first Gay Pride March, that made Stonewall the shot heard 'round the world.

The event had become an idea, the idea that gay people would fight back, would stand up for their rights. And ideas are what change the world.

Michael Denneny has been a distinguished New York City book editor since the 1970s. He founded the literary magazine Christopher Street *in 1976 and launched Stonewall Inn Editions, an imprint at St. Martin's Press, in 1986. He is a member of IndependentEditorsGroup.com.*

STORMÉ DELARVERIE

Did she or didn't she? That is the question. On that warm June night in 1969 as chaos reigned at the Stonewall Inn, was Stormé DeLarverie the "butch lesbian who threw the first punch" that sparked the gay rights movement? Most who knew her would not be at all surprised if that was true. According to long-time friend Lisa Cannistraci, "She literally walked the streets of downtown Manhattan like a gay superhero. She was not to be messed with by any stretch of the imagination."

Born in 1920 in New Orleans to an interracial couple (her mother, who was black, was a servant in her father's house), Stormé started fighting early. "Everybody was jumping on me. . . . If it wasn't because of my father's money it was because of being a negro with a white face, so [my father] told me if I didn't stop running I'd be running the rest of my life. And when I was 15 I stopped running and I haven't run a day since."

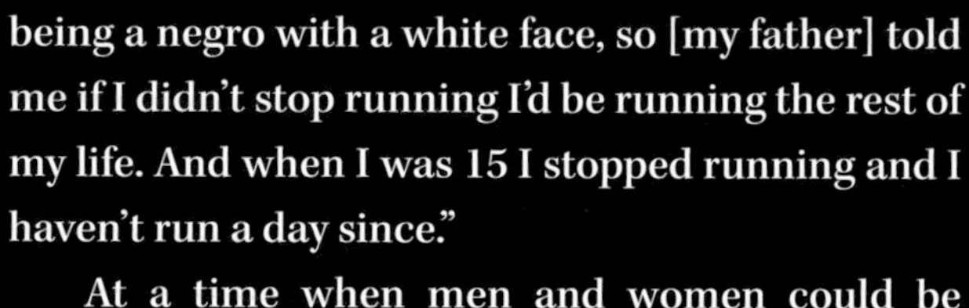

At a time when men and women could be arrested for cross-dressing (as she was several times), she performed as the drag king MC of the Jewel Box Revue, a traveling company of female impersonators, and did not change before going out on the street after work. Her career also included turns as a big band singer, a circus performer, and (some say) as a bodyguard for the mob in Chicago. Later in life (until she was eighty-five-ish), she was "babysitter"/bouncer at many lesbian bars in the West Village. And for twenty-five years she shared her life with a dancer named Diana.

As for the night in question, Cannistraci said, "Nobody knows who threw the first punch, but . . . she told me she did." And in the end, what matters is that someone did. And then . . . everyone did. And, for a time, a gay superhero lived among us.

Above: Stormé DeLarverie in front of the Cubby Hole, New York City, 1986. **Opposite**: Jewel Box Revue MC DeLarverie (center) and three female impersonators at Roberts Show Club, Chicago, Illinois, 1958.

"Those early pickets were scary . . . because there were so few of us who could take the risk of being so public." —Barbara Gittings, gay pioneer

Above: Barbara Gittings, founder of the New York chapter of the Daughters of Bilitis (and considered by many to be the mother of the gay rights movement), with other gay and lesbian activists at the fifth annual Reminder Day protest in Philadelphia, July 4, 1969. **Opposite**: Button collection of the first openly gay candidate for the US Congress (1971, DC) and Washington, DC, Mattachine Society cofounder Frank Kameny.

HOW DARE YOU PRESUME I'M HETEROSEXUAL!

EQUALITY FOR HOMOSEXUALS

COMUNIDAD DE ORGULLO GAY · PUERTO RICO ·

Pa'fuera!

AT THE LEGISLATURE

"...and the Pursuit of Happiness"

TIMES CHANGE PRESS
1023 SIXTH AVE. N.Y.C.
GRAPHIC DESIGN: SU NEGRIN PHOTOGRAPH: PETER HUJAR MANDALA: SUZANNE BEVIER
LET GO LET GO LET GO LET GO
GAY
LIBERATION
GAY TCP-7 © 1970 Su Negrin

WE'RE OUT! SEXUAL FREEDOM FOR ALL (The 1970s)

Though the Stonewall uprising was a completely spontaneous burst of rebellion, it most importantly led to a burst of just the opposite: rebellion through planning and organization. Only weeks after Stonewall, a flyer appeared throughout Greenwich Village that read:

DO YOU THINK HOMOSEXUALS ARE REVOLTING?
YOU BET YOUR SWEET ASS WE ARE
We're going to make a place for ourselves in the revolutionary movement.
We challenge the myths that are screwing up this society.
MEETING: Thursday, July 24th, 6:30 PM at
Alternate U, 69 West 14th Street at Sixth Avenue.

Just a few days after the flyer appeared, on the one-month anniversary of Stonewall, the Mattachine Society held a rally in Washington Square Park. That August, the North American Conference of Homophilc Organizations got together in Kansas City, Missouri. And only a few years later there were well over a thousand gay organizations, ranging from the Lavender Menace (protesting the exclusion of lesbians from the women's movement) to Parents and Friends of Lesbians and Gays (PFLAG) to Lambda Legal (in search of social justice through litigation).

One of the most influential groups of the 1970s, however, was the Gay Activists Alliance (GAA), which adopted an in-your-face approach to the fight for liberation. They formed in December 1969 with the goal of securing "basic human rights, dignity and freedom for all gay people" and were most famous for their street theater "zaps," which were designed to bring attention to the cause through public confrontation. One famous zap happened when two gay couples arrived at New York City's marriage license bureau to get married—a wedding cake topped with grooms in hand—and ended with a takeover. Another time the group dispersed among the crowd in the lobby of an opera that New York mayor John Lindsay was

Opposite: Political poster for the first Gay Pride parade and festival marking the one-year anniversary of Stonewall,1970.

attending then suddenly started shouting "End Police Harassment!" and "Gay Power!" Their goals: fair employment and housing laws, an end to police entrapment and harassment, and more.

And at an Association for the Advancement of Behavior Therapy conference at the New York Hilton in 1972, the Gay Activists Alliance sat in on a lecture about aversion therapy, a technique that used electric shock and nausea-inducing drugs to change sexual orientation. "The room is filled with radical gay liberationists," Dr. Charles Silverstein said to the lecturer in a quiet but firm voice, "and we are here to fight against aversion therapy used against our people. You can talk for fifteen minutes, then we're going to take over the room and tell the audience how gay people are being tortured." That same year, John Fryer appeared in disguise in front of the annual conference of the American Psychiatric Association (APA) in Dallas to reveal that there were a number of gay members of the APA and to bring the issue of homosexuality being mislabeled as a disease to the forefront. The following year, homosexuality was removed from the APA's list of mental illnesses.

"We're becoming militant, and we won't be harassed and degraded any more."

—Martin Robinson,
Gay Activists Alliance

In politics, the women's movement was in full swing, and lesbians—though not always welcome—were joining in droves. Kathy Kozachenko, the first openly gay candidate to run for office in the United States, was elected to the city council of Ann Arbor, Michigan, and Harvey Milk won a seat on the San Francisco board of supervisors.

For the first time gay people were becoming visible in ways that were neither tragic nor criminal, ways that had depth and humanity. At the movies, Peter Finch kissed Murray Head in *Sunday, Bloody Sunday*; in *Cabaret*, loveable Brian slept with Sally and then with Max. On the tennis courts, Martina Navratilova, Billie Jean King, and Renée Richards showed their prowess. And on TV, 10 million viewers watched as Lance Loud came out in an episode of *An American Family*, a twelve-part documentary on PBS.

By the end of the 1970s, due to this convergence of women's liberation, the birth control pill, the growth of LGBTQ+ awareness, and sexual freedom everywhere, the counterculture—for better or worse—began to integrate into pop culture. And in place of the implicit repression of the past there came overt castigation. In 1977, Anita Bryant launched a war cry called Save Our Children, a campaign based on the notion that gay people were out to recruit America's children. Bryant, the born-again-Christian spokesperson for Florida orange juice, ignited a conservative backlash that continues to fuel the anti-gay message of the religious right—and fired up gay rebellion in the process.

Opposite: Gay Liberation Front "gay-in" poster, Los Angeles, c. 1970. **Following pages**: The Gay Liberation Day parade, June 1971.

Gay-in

come together...

reach out and join hands with your brothers and sisters.

at Griffith Park

merry-go-round

April 5

Gay Liberation Front

CHRISTOP
LIBERATIO

VILLAGE CIGARS
NO
RIGHT
TURN
NO
PARKING
ANY
TIME

CLEANERS

GAY
ACTIVISTS
ALLIANCE

BEYOND

Previous pages: A young Vito Russo (striped pants) proudly leads the GAA up Sixth Avenue during the Christopher Street Liberation Day Parade (later called the Gay Pride Parade), 1971. **Above** and **Opposite**: Personal snapshots of the gathering in Central Park on Christopher Street Liberation Day, 1971. **Following pages**: Candlelight commemoration of the Stonewall uprising in Greenwich Village, New York, June 28, 1971.

MARSHA P. JOHNSON

Marsha came into this world on August 24, 1945. Black Marsha is what she called herself at first but eventually she settled on Marsha P. "Pay It No Mind" Johnson (as she once explained to a judge). And though she was from Elizabeth, New Jersey, she once said, "I was no one, nobody, from Nowheresville, until I became a drag queen."

She was also engaged in sex work to survive, was often homeless, was arrested dozens of times, had once been shot, and—understandably—struggled with mental health issues. Susan Stryker, an associate professor of gender and women's studies at the University of Arizona said, "Marsha P. Johnson could be perceived as the most marginalized of people—black, queer, gender-nonconforming, poor." Still, Stryker noted, "You might expect a person in such a position to be fragile, brutalized, beaten down. Instead, Marsha had this joie de vivre, a capacity to find joy in a world of suffering. She channeled it into political action, and did it with a kind of fierceness, grace, and whimsy, with a loopy, absurdist reaction to it all."

> **"Darling, I want my gay rights now."**
>
> —Marsha P. Johnson

She danced to her own drummer for sure, performing with a group called Hot Peaches (by all accounts *not* a gifted singer but mesmerizing nonetheless) and posing for Andy Warhol. Marsha was also a lifelong activist, most notably establishing (with her best friend Sylvia Rivera) Street Transvestite Action Revolutionaries (STAR). Rivera described the group as "for the street gay people, the street homeless people, and anybody that needed help at that time. . . . We didn't want the kids out in the streets hustling." Marsha's great friend and longtime roommate, (the more straight-laced) Randy Wicker, saw STAR as "a bunch of flakey, fucked up transvestites living in a hovel." Nonetheless, in spite of Wicker's views and their oh-so-limited resources, Johnson and Rivera created the first-ever outreach organization and shelter for this community.

Sadly, the body of the much loved and admired Marsha was found floating in the Hudson River on the morning of July 6, 1992. The mystery of her death has never been solved.

Opposite: A still of Marsha P. Johnson, c. 1992, from the 2017 Netflix documentary *The Death and Life of Marsha P. Johnson*

evia

"Before I die, I will see our community given the respect we deserve. . . . I want to go to wherever I go with that in my soul and peacefully say I've finally overcome."

—Sylvia Rivera, gay liberation and transgender rights activist

Above: Marchers in the1973 Christopher Street Liberation Day parade. **Opposite**: Marsha P. Johnson and Sylvia Rivera (right) marching in the 1973 Christopher Street Liberation Day parade.

I'M FROM Woodmere N.Y.
SUPERVISOR
HARVEY
MILK

HOPE

Speech by Harvey Milk at San Francisco's Gay Freedom Day Parade, June 25, 1978. Milk was assassinated in November of the same year.

My name is Harvey Milk and I'm here to recruit you.

I've been saving this one for years. It's a political joke. I can't help it—I've got to tell it. I've never been able to talk to this many political people before, so if I tell you nothing else you may be able to go home laughing a bit.

This ocean liner was going across the ocean and it sank. And there was one little piece of wood floating, and three people swam to it, and they realized only one person could hold on to it. So they had a little debate about which was the person. It so happened the three people were the pope, the president, and Mayor Daley. The pope said he was titular head of one of the great religions of the world and he was spiritual adviser to many, many millions, and he went on and pontificated, and they thought it was a good argument. Then the president said he was leader of the largest and most powerful nation of the world. What takes place in this country affects the whole world, and they thought that was a good argument. And Mayor Daley said he was mayor of the backbone of the United States, and what took place in Chicago affected the world, and what took place in the archdiocese of Chicago affected Catholicism. And they thought that was a good argument. So they did it the democratic way and voted. And Daley won, seven to two.

About six months ago, Anita Bryant in her speaking to God said that the drought in California was because of the gay people. On November 9, the day after I got elected, it started to rain. On the day I got sworn in, we walked to City Hall and it was kinda nice, and as soon as I said the words "I do," it started to rain again. It's been raining since then, and the people of San Francisco figure the only way to stop it is to do a recall petition. That's a local joke.

So much for that. Why are we here? Why are gay people here? And what's happening? What's happening to me is the antithesis of what you read about in the

Opposite: Supervisor Harvey Milk and his campaign manager Anne Kronenberg in Milk's last San Francisco Gay and Lesbian Freedom Day Parade, June 25, 1978.

papers and what you hear about on the radio. You hear about and read about this movement to the right. That we must band together and fight back this movement to the right. And I'm here to go ahead and say that what you hear and read is what they want you to think because it's not happening. The major media in this country had talked about the movement to the right so much that they've got even us thinking that way. Because they want the legislators to think that there is indeed a movement to the right and that the Congress and the legislators and the city councils will start to move to the right the way the major media want them. So they keep on talking about this move to the right.

So let's look at 1977 and see if there was indeed a move to the right. In 1977, gay people had their rights taken away from them in Miami. But you must remember that in the week before Miami and the week after that, the word *homosexual* or *gay* appeared in every single newspaper in this nation in articles both pro and con. In every radio station, in every TV station and every household. For the first time in the history of the world, everybody was talking about it, good or bad. Unless you have dialogue, unless you open the walls of dialogue, you can never reach to change people's opinion. In those two weeks, more good and bad, but *more* about the words *homosexual* and *gay* was written than probably in the history of mankind. Once you have dialogue starting, you know you can break down the prejudice. In 1977 we saw a dialogue start. In 1977, we saw a gay person elected in San Francisco. In 1977 we saw the state of Mississippi decriminalize marijuana. In 1977, we saw the convention of conventions in Houston. And I want to know where the movement to the right is happening.

What that is is a record of what happened last year. What we must do is make sure that 1978 continues the movement that is really happening that the media don't want you to know about, that is the movement to the left. It's up to CDC to put the pressures on Sacramento—not to just bring flowers to Sacramento—but to break down the walls and the barriers so the movement to the left continues and progress continues in the nation. We have before us coming up several issues we must speak out on. Probably the most important issue outside the Briggs—which we will come to—but we do know what will take place this June. We know there's an issue on the ballot called Jarvis-Gann. We hear the taxpayers talk about it on both sides. But what you don't hear is that it's probably the most racist issue on the ballot in a long time. In the city and county of San Francisco, if it passes and we indeed have to lay off people, who will they be? The last in, not the first in, and who are the last in but the minorities? Jarvis-Gann is a racist issue. We must address that issue. We must not talk away from it. We must not allow them to talk about the money it's going to save, because look at who's going to save the money and who's going to get hurt.

We also have another issue that we've started in some of the north counties and I hope in some of the south counties it continues. In San Francisco elections we're asking—at least we hope to ask—that the US government put pressure on the closing of the South African consulate. That must happen. There is a major difference between an embassy in Washington, which is a diplomatic bureau, and a consulate in major cities. A consulate is there for one reason only—to promote business, economic gains, tourism, investment. And every time you have business going to South Africa, you're promoting a regime that's offensive.

In the city of San Francisco, if everyone of 51 percent of that city were to go to South Africa, they would be treated as second-class citizens. That is an offense to the people of San Francisco, and I hope all my colleagues up there will take every step we can to close down that consulate and hope that people in other parts of the state follow us in that lead. The battles must be started someplace, and CDC is the greatest place to start the battles.

I know we are pressed for time, so I'm going to cover just one more little point. That is to understand why it is important that gay people run for office and that gay people get elected. I know there are many people in this room who are running for central committee who are gay. I encourage you. There's a major reason why. If my non-gay friends and supporters in this room understand it, they'll probably understand why I've run so often before I finally made it. You see, right now, there's a controversy going on in the convention about the governor. Is he speaking out enough? Is he strong enough for gay rights? And there is a controversy, and for us to say it is not would be foolish. Some people are satisfied and some people are not.

You see, there is a major difference—and it remains a vital difference—between a friend and a gay person, a friend in office and a gay person in office. Gay people have been slandered nationwide. We've been tarred and we've been bruised with the picture of pornography. In Dade County, we were accused of child molestation. It's not enough anymore just to have friends represent us. No matter how good that friend may be.

The black community made up its mind to that a long time ago. That the myths against blacks can only be dispelled by electing black leaders, so the black community could be judged by the leaders and not by the myths or black criminals. The Spanish community must not be judged by Latin criminals or myths. The Asian community must not be judged by Asian criminals or myths. The Italian community should not be judged by the mafia myths. And the time has come when the gay community must not be judged by our criminals and myths.

Like every other group, we must be judged by our leaders and by those who are themselves gay, those who are visible. For invisible, we remain in limbo—a myth, a person with no parents, no brothers, no sisters, no friends who are straight, no important positions in employment. A tenth of a nation supposedly composed of stereotypes and would-be seducers of children—and no offense meant to the stereotypes. But today, the black community is not judged by its friends, but by its black legislators and leaders. And we must give people the chance to judge us by our leaders and legislators. A gay person in office can set a tone, can command respect not only from the larger community, but from the young people in our own community who need both examples and hope.

The first gay people we elect must be strong. They must not be content to sit in the

I think it's time that we have many legislators who are gay and proud of that fact and do not have to remain in the closet.

back of the bus. They must not be content to accept pablum. They must be above wheeling and dealing. They must be—for the good of all of us—independent, unbought. The anger and the frustration that some of us feel is because we are misunderstood, and friends can't feel that anger and frustration. They can sense it in us, but they can't feel it. Because a friend has never gone through what is known as coming out. I will never forget what it was like coming out and having nobody to look up toward. I remember the lack of hope—and our friends can't fulfill that.

I can't forget the looks on faces of people who've lost hope. Be they gay, be they seniors, be they blacks looking for an almost-impossible job, be they Latins trying to explain their problems and aspirations in a tongue that's foreign to them. I personally will never forget that people are more important than buildings. I use the word "I" because I'm proud. I stand here tonight in front of my gay sisters, brothers, and friends because I'm proud of you. I think it's time that we have many legislators who are gay and proud of that fact and do not have to remain in the closet. I think that a gay person, up front, will not walk away from a responsibility and be afraid of being tossed out of office. After Dade County, I walked among the angry and the frustrated night after night and I looked at their faces. And in San Francisco, three days before Gay Pride Day, a person was killed just because he was gay. And that night, I walked among the sad and the frustrated at City Hall in San Francisco and later that night as they lit candles on Castro Street and stood in silence, reaching out for some symbolic thing that would give them hope. These were strong people, people whose faces I knew from the shop, the streets, meetings, and people who I never saw before but I knew. They were strong, but even they needed hope.

And the young gay people in the Altoona, Pennsylvanias, and the Richmond, Minnesotas, who are coming out and hear Anita Bryant on television and her story. The only thing they have to look forward to is hope. And you have to give them hope. Hope for a better world, hope for a better tomorrow, hope for a better place to come to if the pressures at home are too great. Hope that all will be all right. Without hope, not only gays, but the blacks, the seniors, the handicapped, the "us"es, the "us"es will give up. And if you help elect to the central committee and other offices more gay people, that gives a green light to all who feel disenfranchised, a green light to move forward. It means hope to a nation that has given up, because if a gay person makes it, the doors are open to everyone.

So if there is a message I have to give, it is that if I've found one overriding thing about my personal election, it's the fact that if a gay person can be elected, it's a green light. And you and you and you, you have to give people hope. Thank you very much.

HARVEY MILK

In November 1977, the news spread from California to upstate New York: San Francisco had elected a gay man to its board of supervisors. Harvey Milk became one of the first openly gay elected officials in the United States, but his victory was no surprise—at least to him. For five years he had considered himself an "unofficial supervisor," the go-to guy in the Castro District for getting things done. Even through three previous, unsuccessful campaigns, Milk was a political mainstay with an ever-growing constituency who often showed up at his camera shop with requests. "After I ran the first time," he said in 1977, "the store became a political hangout for people with problems who kept getting the runaround from city officials. It's been that way ever since."

Born in 1930 on Long Island, Milk came to politics after a long string of occupations, from public school math teacher and Navy diver on a rescue submarine to insurance statistician, Broadway production assistant, and Wall Street broker. His Navy officer career had ended in 1955 when official questions about his sexual orientation forced him to resign.

Milk was a popular supervisor who dedicated himself to issues concerning all his constituents. Day care centers, low-cost housing, anti-discrimination, libraries,community policing—his leadership impacted every corner of his district. His speeches inspired gay Americans across the country to come out and live their authentic lives, calling them to end the "conspiracy of silence" and "fight the lies, the myths, the distortions."

A year after taking office, Milk and George Moscone, the Democratic San Francisco mayor he supported, were assassinated by a former member of the board of supervisors. Milk had been keenly aware that his life could end violently, since he received daily death threats. In his tape-recorded will, he made a statement that remains a testament to his spirit: "If a bullet should enter my brain, let that bullet destroy every closet door."

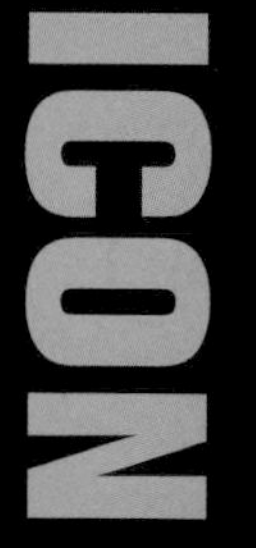

Above: Selection of political buttons from Harvey Milk's career.

"In 1978, when I thought of creating a flag for the gay movement, there was no other international symbol for us than the pink triangle, which the Nazis used to identify homosexuals in concentration camps. Even though the pink triangle was and still is a powerful symbol, it was very much forced upon us. I almost instantly thought of using the rainbow. To me, it was the only thing that could really express our diversity, beauty, and our joy. I was astounded nobody had thought of making a rainbow flag before because it seemed like such an obvious symbol for us."

—Gilbert Baker, artist and rights activist

Opposite: Image of the original gay flag designed in 1978 by Gilbert Baker in reaction to the assassination of Harvey Milk. Baker assigned specific meaning to each of the original eight colors: violet = spirit, indigo = serenity, turquoise = magic/art, green = nature, yellow = sunlight, orange = healing, red = life, hot pink = sex.

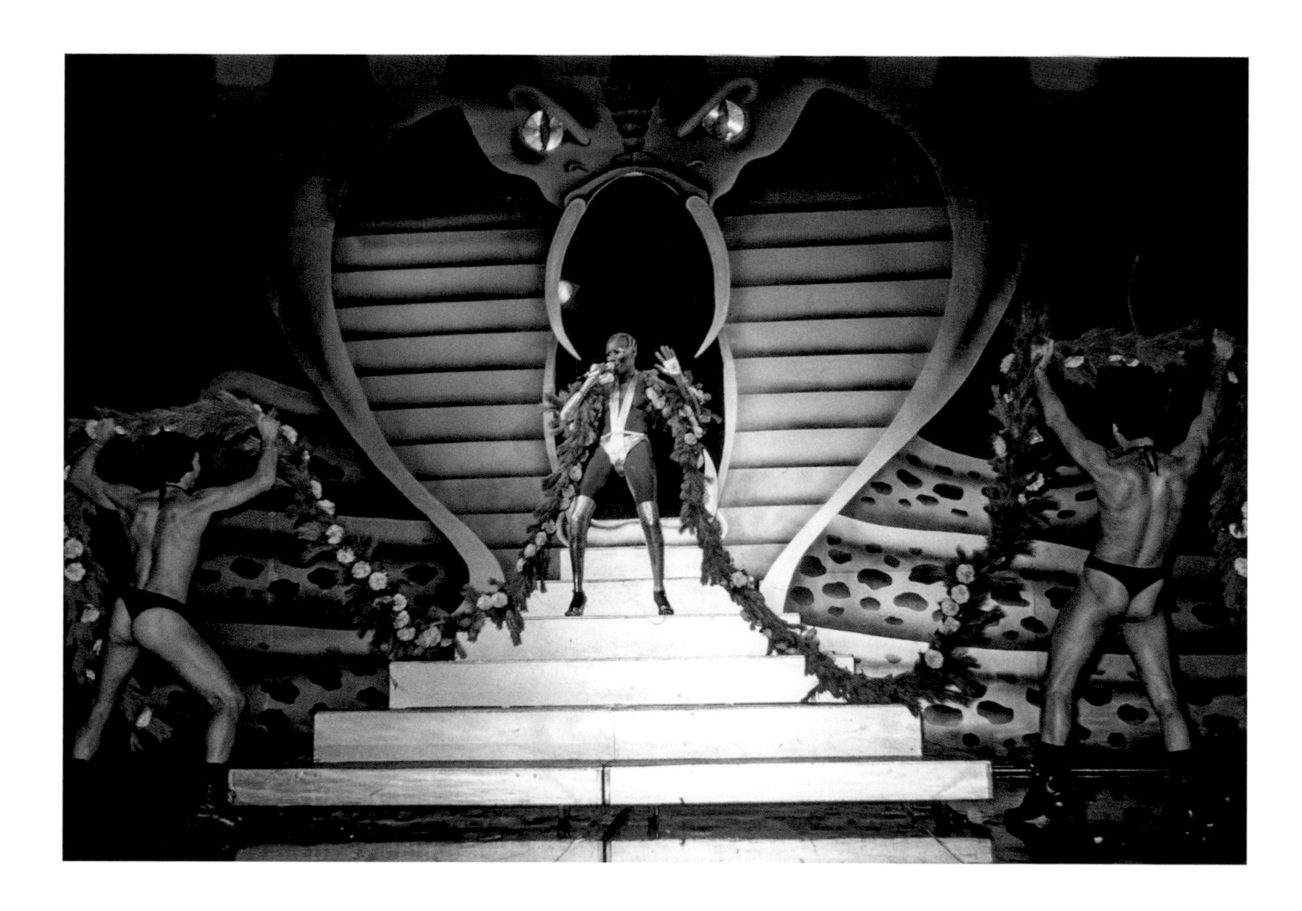

"Popular culture was suffused with stunning displays of homosexual burlesque: the music of Queen, the costumes of the Village People, the flamboyance of Elton John's debut, the advertising of Calvin Klein, and the intoxication of disco itself, a gay creation that became emblematic of an entire heterosexual era." —Andrew Sullivan

Opposite: The "Queen of Disco," Sylvester (born Sylvester James Jr.), in the 1970s. He was known for his flamboyant and androgynous appearance and falsetto singing voice. His hit song "You Make Me Feel (Mighty Real)" became a worldwide gay anthem. Sylvester died from complications arising from the AIDS virus in 1988, leaving all future royalties from his work to San Francisco–based HIV/AIDS charities. **Above**: Grace Jones at Studio 54, January 1978. Music and pop culture writer Barry Walters described her in the 1970s "as queer as a relatively straight person could get. Her image celebrated blackness and subverted gender norms; she presented something we had never seen before in pop performance."

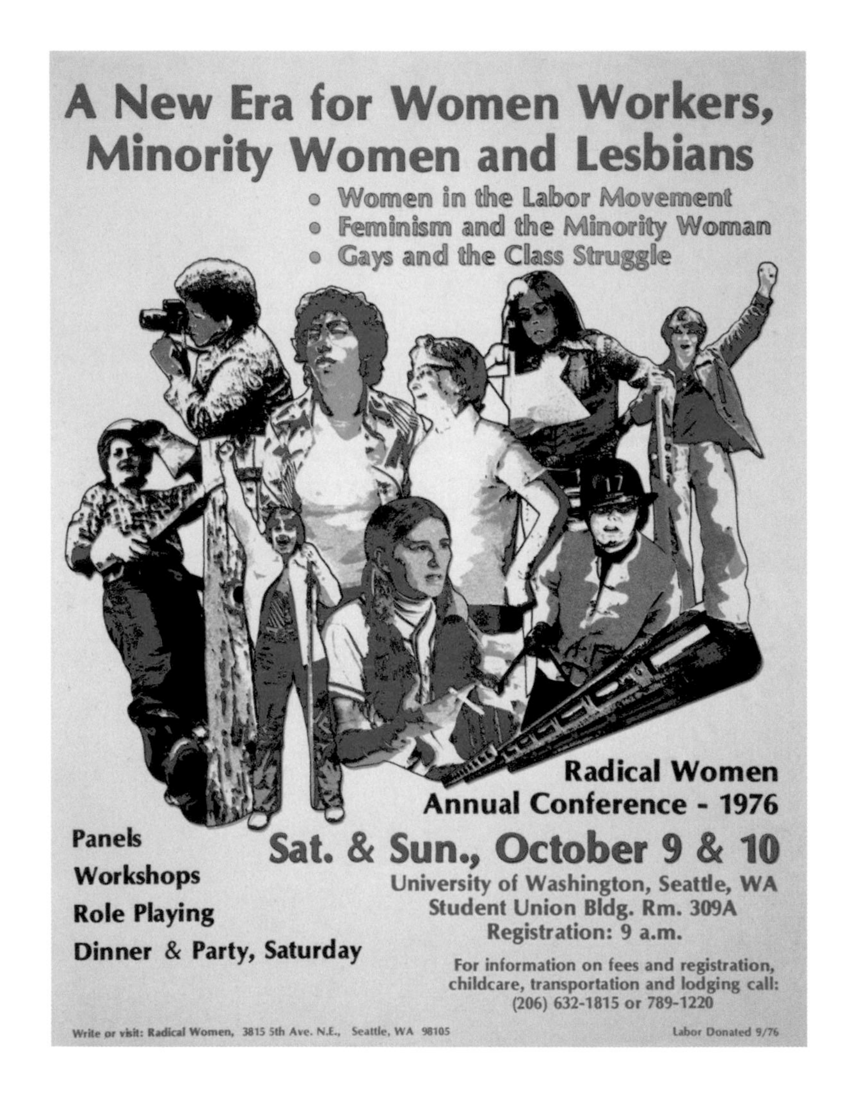

"What made us soar was just this amazing women's movement that was emerging. No matter what any woman ever says today it was chock-full of lesbians."

—Elizabeth Birch, human rights activist

Above: Poster for the University of Washington Radical Women's Annual Conference, 1976. **Opposite**: Transsexual Renée Richards competing at the US Open Tennis Tournament at Flushing Meadows, New York, September 1979.

PART 3
. . . GET USED TO IT!

This Political Scandal Must Be Investigated!

54% of people with AIDS in NYC are Black or Hispanic... AIDS is the No. 1 killer of women between the ages of 24 and 29 in NYC...

By 1991, more people will have died of AIDS than in the *entire* Vietnam War...What is Reagan's *real* policy on AIDS?

Genocide of all Non-whites, Non-males, and Non-heterosexuals?...

SILENCE = DEATH

A CRISIS BRINGS EVERYBODY OUT
(The 1980s)

RARE CANCER SEEN IN 41 HOMOSEXUALS—so reported the *New York Times* on July 3, 1981, in a single-column piece on page A20. The article continued, "The cause of the outbreak is unknown. . . . Dr. Alvin E. Friedman-Kien of New York University Medical Center, one of the investigators, described the appearance of the outbreak as 'rather devastating.'"

And the movement had come so far. By the end of the 1970s, "gay invisibility was just a distant memory," Charles Kaiser notes in his book *The Gay Metropolis*, "with the proliferation of gay characters on network TV sitcoms and frequent political battles over gay civil rights laws. . . . By 1980, in response to the growing clamor for equality, 120 of the largest corporations . . . had adopted personnel policies prohibiting discrimination on the basis of sexual orientation, and 40 towns and cities had passed similar laws or issued executive orders. . . . Twenty-two states had ended all restrictions on sexual relations between consenting adults, and on the tenth anniversary of Stonewall, seventeen-year-old Randy Rohl took twenty-year-old Grady Quinn to the senior prom in Sioux Falls, South Dakota."

But as the 1980s began, the preppy look had replaced bell-bottoms and love beads, the religious right was gaining momentum, Ronald Reagan was elected to the White House, and the country took a conservative turn. Then AIDS—an adversary of mammoth proportions—came out of nowhere. While an extraordinary response would emerge from the community and astonishing gains would eventually follow, there was unimaginable pain first.

Previous pages: Pride parade participants, New York City, 2016. **Opposite**: ACT UP poster, 1987. **Above**: A delegate at the 1980 Democratic convention in New York.

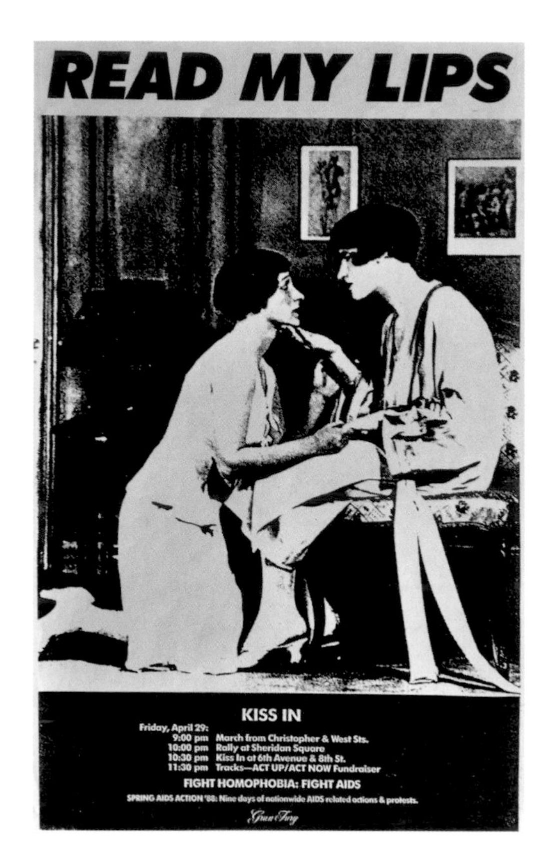

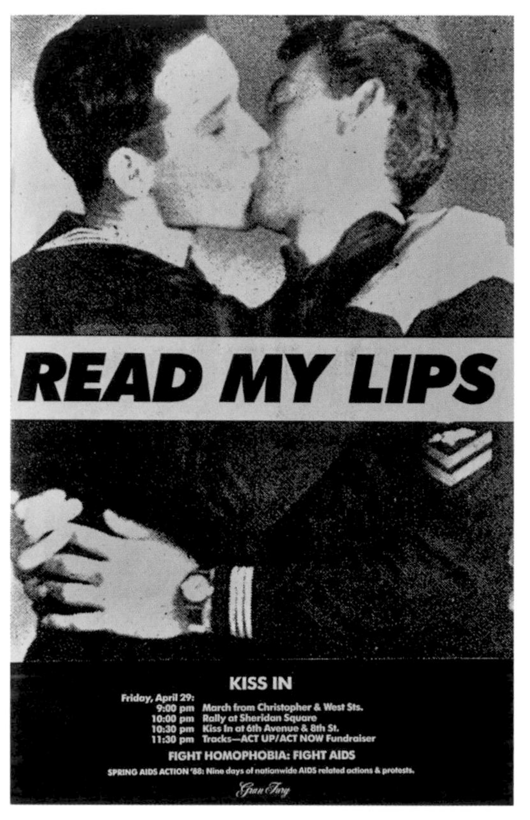

This exchange is from an October 15, 1982 White House Press Briefing:

REPORTER: Larry, does the president have any reaction to the announcement . . . that A-I-D-S is now an epidemic [with] over 600 cases?

WHITE HOUSE PRESS SECRETARY LARRY SPEAKS: What's AIDS? [. . .] I don't have it, do you? *(laughter)*

REPORTER: In other words, the White House looks on this as a great joke? . . . Does the president, does anybody in the White House know about this epidemic, Larry?

LARRY SPEAKS: I don't think so.

Not only was the community being ravaged by a mysterious disease, but the government was purposefully turning a blind eye. Nearly five years would pass—and tens of thousands would die—before the president addressed the problem publicly. But as Kaiser wrote of setbacks and defeats, "Such reversals proved once again how much the movement could be strengthened by adversity."

"We have to start being powerful or we are going to die," Larry Kramer recounted later in the 2011 HBO documentary *Vito*. "It is up to us." And so in 1981, he asked Friedman-Kien to come to his apartment and speak to a group of gay men about the disease. The following year Kramer cofounded Gay Men's Health Crisis, and in 1987 started the AIDS Coalition to Unleash Power (ACT UP)—which *Time* magazine called "the most effective health activist [group] in history." Dozens of other organizations were created from within the community to deal with the disaster, and though AIDS overwhelmingly struck gay men, lesbians were critical players in education and activism. ACT UP member Alexis Danzig recalled that women were "highly skilled in organizing and provided essential tactical skills, including nonviolent civil disobedience trainings." She and Marion Banzhaf were among those who helped speed up drug approvals, which saved millions of lives, and journalist Ann Northrop was key in organizing highly effective ACT UP protests.

Awareness among and support from the straight community came as the face of the disease became familiar. When movie star and matinee idol Rock Hudson came forward in July 1985 announcing he had the disease—the first major public figure to do so—AIDS stories in the media more than tripled over the following six months. People began to realize both the extent of the disease and the extent of the LGBTQ community. It wasn't the odd celebrity or a whispered-about neighbor down the block who was gay. Suddenly it was brothers and fathers and uncles and cousins and best friends. So many outed by a visible, swift, and devastating catastrophe.

Opposite: Posters designed by Avram Finkelstein for the AIDS activist artist collective Gran Fury, 1988. **Right**: At the London Pride march, 1988.

ACT UP

THE NORMAL HEART

by Larry Kramer

(MICKEY and CRAIG leave. DR. EMMA BROOKNER comes in from her office. She is in a motorized wheelchair. She is in her mid-to-late thirties.)

EMMA: Who are you?

NED: I'm Ned Weeks. I spoke with you on the phone after the *Times* article.

EMMA: You're the writer fellow who's scared. I'm scared, too. I hear you've got a big mouth.

NED: Is big mouth a symptom?

EMMA: No, a cure. Come on in. Take your clothes off.

(Lights up on an examining table, center stage. NED starts to undress.)

NED: Dr. Brookner, what's happening?

EMMA: I don't know.

NED: In just a couple of minutes you told two people I know something. The article said there isn't any cure.

EMMA: Not even any good clues yet. All I know is this disease is the most insidious killer I've ever seen or studied or heard about. And I think we're seeing only the tip of the iceberg. And I'm afraid it's on the rampage. I'm frightened nobody important is going to give a damn because it seems to be happening mostly to gay men. Who cares if a faggot dies? Does it occur to you to do anything about it. Personally?

NED: Me?

Opposite: Playwright, novelist, and journalist Larry Kramer at his home in New York's Greenwich Village, November 29, 1989. Kramer is the founder of and one of the principal voices in the AIDS Coalition to Unleash Power, or ACT UP.

EMMA: Somebody's got to do something.

NED: Wouldn't it be better coming from you?

EMMA: Doctors are extremely conservative; they try to stay out of anything that smells political, and this smells. Bad. As soon as you start screaming you get treated like a nut case. Maybe you know that. And then you're ostracized and rendered worthless, just when you need cooperation most. Take off your socks.

(NED, in his undershorts, is now sitting on the examining table. EMMA will now examine him, his skin particularly, starting with the bottoms of his feet, feeling his lymph glands, looking at his scalp, into his mouth . . .)

NED: Nobody listens for very long anyway. There's a new disease of the month every day.

EMMA: This hospital sent its report of our first cases to the medical journals over a year ago. The *New England Journal of Medicine* has finally published it, and last week, which brought you running, the *Times* ran something on some inside page. Very inside: page twenty. If you remember, Legionnaires' disease, toxic shock, they both hit the front page of the *Times* the minute they happened. And stayed there until somebody did something. The front page of the *Times* has a way of inspiring action. Lie down.

NED: They won't even use the word "gay" unless it's in a direct quote. To them we're still homosexuals. That's like still calling blacks Negroes. The *Times* has always had trouble writing about anything gay.

EMMA: Then how is anyone going to know what's happening? And what precautions to take? Someone's going to have to tell the gay population fast.

NED: You've been living with this for over a year? Where's the mayor? Where's the Health Department'?

EMMA: They know about it. You have a commissioner of health who got burned with the swine flu epidemic, declaring an emergency when there wasn't one. The government appropriated $150 million for that mistake. You have a mayor who's a bachelor and, I assume, afraid of being perceived as too friendly to anyone gay. And who is also out to protect a billion-dollar-a-year tourist industry. He's not about to tell the world there's an epidemic menacing his city. And don't ask me about the president. Is Mayor Koch gay?

NED: If he is, like J. Edgar Hoover, who would want him?

EMMA: Have you had any of the symptoms?

NED: I've had most of the sexually transmitted diseases the article said come first. A lot of us have. You don't know what it's been like since the sexual revolution hit this country. It's been crazy, gay or straight.

EMMA: What makes you think I don't know? Any fever, weight loss, night sweats, diarrhea, swollen glands, white patches in your mouth, loss of energy, shortness of breath, chronic cough?

NED: No. But those could happen with a lot of things, couldn't they?

EMMA: And purple lesions. Sometimes. Which is what I'm looking for. It's a cancer.

Above: Larry Kramer with his friend author and activist Vito Russo, c. 1990.

There seems to be a strange reaction in the immune system. It's collapsed. Won't work. Won't fight. Which is what it's supposed to do. So most of the diseases my guys are coming down with—and there are some very strange ones—are caused by germs that wouldn't hurt a baby, not a baby in New York City, anyway. Unfortunately, the immune system is the system we know least about. So where is this big mouth I hear you've got?

NED: I have more of a bad temper than a big mouth.

EMMA: Nothing wrong with that. Plenty to get angry about. Health is a political issue. Everyone's entitled to good medical care. If you're not getting it, you've got to fight for it. Turn around. One of my staff told me you were well known in the gay world and not afraid to say what you think. Is that true? I can't find any gay leaders. I tried calling several gay organizations. No one ever calls me back. Is anyone out there?

NED: There aren't any organizations strong enough to be useful, no. Dr. Brookner, nobody with a brain gets involved in gay politics. It's filled with the great unwashed radicals of any counterculture. That's why there aren't any leaders the majority will follow. Anyway, you're talking to the wrong person. What I think is politically incorrect.

EMMA: Why?

NED: Gay is good to that crowd, no matter what. There's no room for criticism, looking at ourselves critically.

EMMA: What's your main criticism?

NED: I hate how we play victim, when many of us, most of us, don't have to.

EMMA: Then you're exactly what's needed now.

NED: Nobody ever listens. We're not exactly a bunch that knows how to play follow the leader.

EMMA: Maybe they're just waiting for somebody to lead them.

NED: We are. What group isn't?

EMMA: You can get dressed. I can't find what I'm looking for.

NED: *(jumping down and starting to dress)* Needed? Needed for what? What is it exactly you're trying to get me to do?

EMMA: Tell gay men to stop having sex.

NED: What?

EMMA: Someone has to. Why not you?

NED: It is a preposterous request.

EMMA: It only sounds harsh. Wait a few more years, it won't sound so harsh.

NED: Do you realize that you are talking about millions of men who have singled out promiscuity to be their principal political agenda, the one they'd die before abandoning? How do you deal with that?

EMMA: Tell them they may die.

NED: You tell them!

EMMA: Are you saying you guys can't relate to each other in a nonsexual way?

NED: It's more complicated than that. For a lot of guys, it's not easy to meet each other in any other way. It's a way of connecting—which becomes an addiction. And then they're caught in the web of peer pressure to perform and perform. Are you sure this is spread by having sex?

EMMA: Long before we isolated the hepatitis viruses we knew about the diseases they caused and how they got around. I think I'm right about this. I am seeing more cases each week than the week before. I figure that by the end of the year the number will be doubling every six months. That's something over a thousand cases by next June. Half of them will be dead. Your two friends I've just diagnosed? One of them will be dead. Maybe both of them.

NED: And you want me to tell every gay man in New York to stop having sex?

EMMA: Who said anything about just New York?

NED: You want me to tell every gay man across the country—

EMMA: Across the world! That's the only way this disease will stop spreading.

NED: Dr. Brookner, isn't that just a tiny bit unrealistic?

EMMA: Mr. Weeks, if having sex can kill you, doesn't anybody with half a brain stop fucking? But perhaps you've never lost anything. Good-bye.

VITO RUSSO

"Life is full of injustice, and some people it bothers and some people it doesn't. Me, it bothers. I don't think I could live any other way."

Vito Russo found his calling as a gay-rights activist in the earliest days of the movement. Growing up Catholic in New York and coming of age in the 1960s, he embraced his sexuality and rejected the Church's stance on homosexuality—but it took a tragedy to ignite his activism. The death of Diego Viñales during the police raid of a Manhattan gay bar in March 1970 had stoked protests from the fledgling Gay Activists Alliance (GAA). As Russo walked by the demonstration, he learned that Viñales had jumped out of a window to escape and been impaled on an iron fence. The GAA leaflet's message—"No matter how you look at it, Diego Viñales was pushed!"—made Russo aware that society was to blame—the events of gay and lesbian lives were political. "That was my turning point," he said.

After witnessing the Stonewall rebellion, Russo took on a fevered mission to enlighten America about gay and lesbian lives. At the same time, his work as a film scholar focused on Hollywood's characterizations of gays and lesbians and produced the groundbreaking book *The Celluloid Closet: Homosexuality in the Movies* (1981). In 1983, he brought gay issues to the public airwaves with the launch of *Our Time* on WNYC-TV. Two years later, after being diagnosed with human immunodeficiency virus (HIV), Russo became a cofounder of ACT UP, and when his partner died of AIDS in 1986, he cofounded the media watchdog group the Gay and Lesbian Alliance Against Defamation (GLAAD).

The world lost Russo to AIDS in 1990, when he was forty-four. He remains a legend, honored with GLAAD's Vito Russo Media Award; the 1996 documentary *The Celluloid Closet*; Michael Schiavi's 2011 biography, *Celluloid Activist*; and the 2011 documentary about his life, *Vito*.

Above: Film historian and writer Vito Russo at the Hyde Park Plaza Hotel, London, February 17, 1986.

ACT UP

By the spring of 1987, acquired immune deficiency syndrome (AIDS) had killed roughly twenty thousand people in the United States, mostly gay men. Larry Kramer, the Oscar-nominated screenwriter and playwright who had cofounded the Gay Men's Health Crisis (GMHC) five years earlier, was frustrated that the organization had no political clout. While the GMHC provided much-needed services to AIDS patients, it had no impact on a government that refused to address the epidemic. Kramer channeled his trademark fury over the social injustice around AIDS into forming a new organization committed to political action.

On March 24, 1987, Kramer's newly founded AIDS Coalition to Unleash Power (ACT UP) held its first protest on Wall Street, disrupting morning traffic to revolt against drug company profiteering and demand better access to experimental drugs. That same month, Burroughs Wellcome had announced its release of AZT, the first AIDS drug, with a $10,000 price tag for a year's supply. The next action proved how well ACT UP's in-your-face strategy worked. When demonstrators in suits and ties descended upon Burroughs Wellcome headquarters in North Carolina, they warned executives to lower the price or they would escalate their protests. "The whole industry was watching and were horrified," said ACT UP member Peter Staley. Forty-eight hours later, the company reduced the price by 20 percent.

These early successes solidified ACT UP's role as a force for change. ACT UP members, according to *Time* magazine, became the "most effective health activists in history, pressuring drug companies, government agencies and other powers that stood in their way to find better treatments for people with AIDS."

By 2017, Kramer was still convinced that hard-hitting activism must continue. "We have people running this government who hate us, and have said they hate us," he said. "The fight's never over."

Above: Poster created by Silence = Death project, a radical queer activist group founded by Avram Finkelstein, Brian Howard, Oliver Johnston, Charles Kreloff, Chris Lione, and Jorge Socarrás. **Opposite**: ACT UP die-in at the Food and Drug Administration headquarters in Rockville, Maryland, in demand of a shorter drug approval process and other key demands, October 11, 1988.

HAPPEN
HERE
GUILTY
"...If I had a bout of pneumocystis... I would go for what is available on the street..."
Anthony Fauci
National Institutes of Health
SILENCE = DEATH
TIME ISN'T THE ONLY THING THE FDA IS KILLING
GUILTY
"Testing is more cost-effective than treatment."
George Bush
Presidential Candidate
5600
DEAD FROM LACK DEXTRAN SULFATE
FOR THE
OF THE
FDA
R.I.P. Killed By The F.D.A.
BY THE SYSTEM
ACT UP

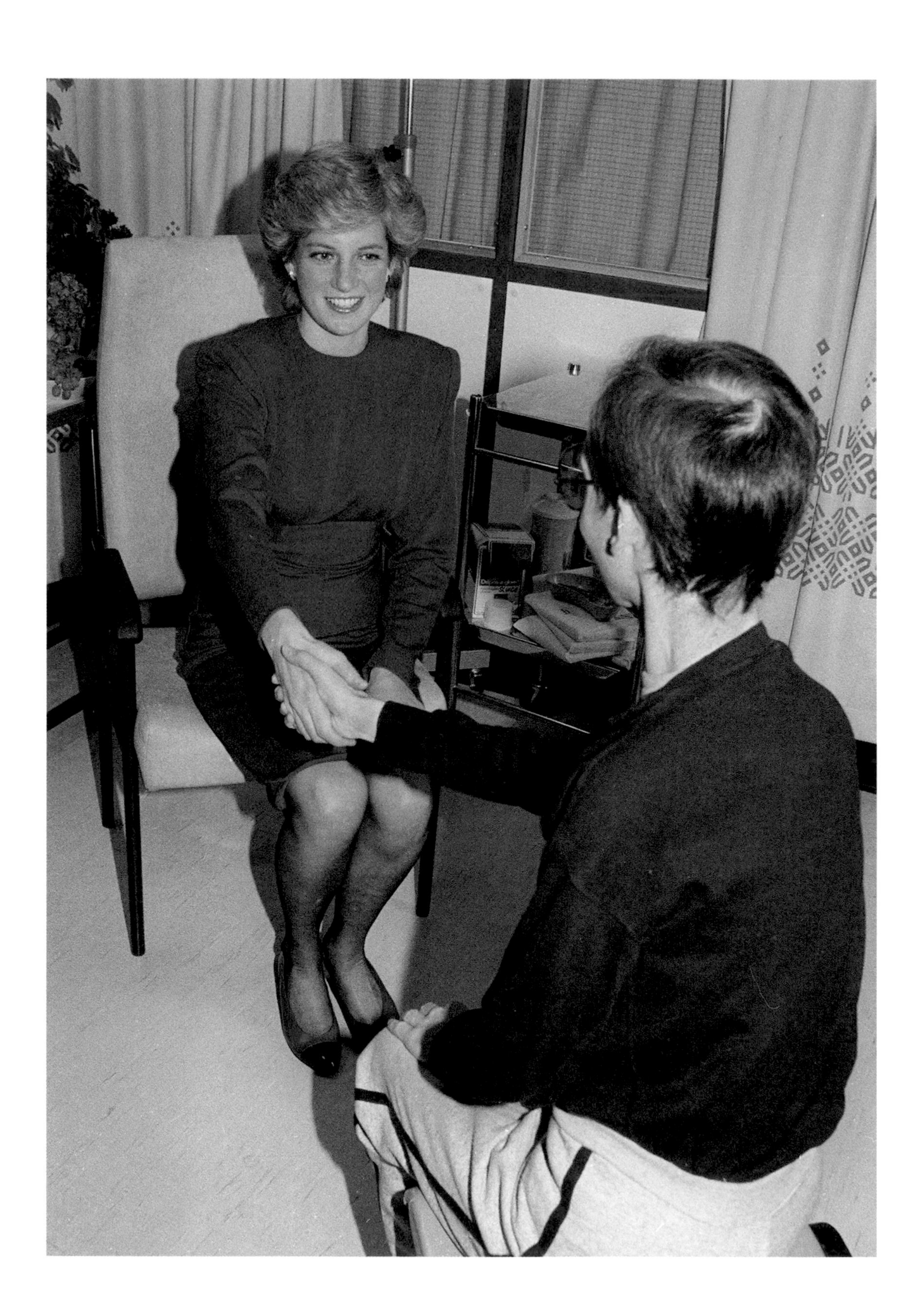

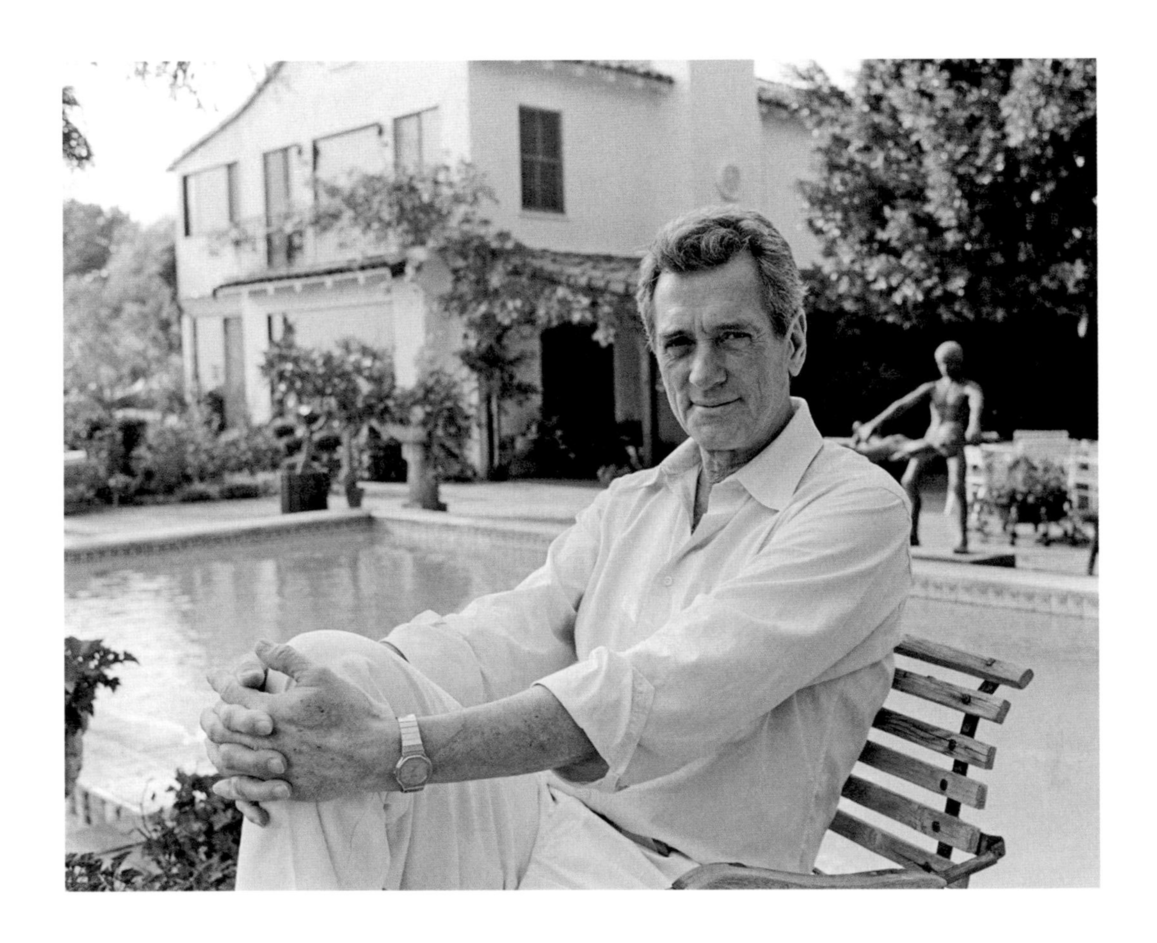

"I was with him the night before [he died]. . . . We laughed about making chocolate martinis. He was just skin and bones. And I thought, I am going to do everything in my living power to get at this disease and kill it by its throat." —Elizabeth Taylor

Opposite: Diana, Princess of Wales, becomes the first person to touch an AIDS patient bare-handed in his private room at Middlesex Hospital, London, April 19, 1987. The thirty-two-year-old patient requested that he not be identified. **Above**: Matinee idol Rock Hudson at home in Hollywood, November 8, 1984. In July 1985 Hudson announced he had AIDS; he was the first major public figure to do so. He died less than three months later, leaving $250,000 in his will to help set up the American Foundation for AIDS Research (amfAR). His close friend, *Giant* costar, and drinking buddy, Elizabeth Taylor, served as the organization's founding national chairperson.

THE AIDS MEMORIAL QUILT

Each panel is three by six feet, the size of a grave. But the celebration of life in every word, color, texture, and strip of fabric reflects the spirit of a loved one who will never be forgotten.

Gay rights activist and cofounder of the San Francisco AIDS Foundation Cleve Jones had envisioned the AIDS Memorial Quilt in a split-second moment of creative clarity. During the 1985 candlelight march commemorating San Francisco's slain Harvey Milk and George Moscone, Jones lamented that the suffering and death of his city's one thousand AIDS victims was still invisible. At the end of the march, he looked up at the façade of the Federal Building, covered with posters listing the names of AIDS victims. The sight struck him as "some kind of odd quilt" like those his grandmother and great-grandmother had sewn back in Indiana.

The traditional symbol felt right. "I could just see it in my head so clearly, how it would look stretched out on the mall," Jones said. "I could see how it could work as therapy, for people who were grieving, as a tool for the media to understand the lives that are behind the statistics, as a weapon to shame the government for its inaction."

Two years later, Jones and a group of supporters founded the Names Project Foundation to create a large memorial to remember those who had died. Word spread and panels flooded in from across the country, handmade by the families, friends, and coworkers of AIDS victims. The first Quilt display was scheduled for October 11, 1987, to coincide with the National March on Washington for Lesbian and Gay Rights. National and international tours ensued, and by 2018, the Quilt had grown to more than forty-eight thousand panels, weighing fifty-four tons. Money raised from the displays has supported AIDS service organizations across North America.

The largest work of community folk art in the world, the Quilt has brought healing, unity, and compassion to millions.

ICON

Above: Cleve Jones in front of a panel from the AIDS Quilt, 2001. **Opposite**: The 1,920-panel Aids Quilt was displayed for the first time on the National Mall in Washington, DC, 1987. **Following pages**: The Quilt on tour in Denver, 1988.

RAIN

TWO STEPS FORWARD . . .
(The 1990s)

Justin, Oliver (*Absolutely Fabulous*); Bianca Montgomery (*All My Children*); Samantha (*Beverly Hills 90210*); Willow Rosenberg (*Buffy the Vampire Slayer*); Dr. Dennis Hancock (*Chicago Hope*); Jack McPhee (*Dawson's Creek*); Colin (*EastEnders*); Ellen (*Ellen*); Dr. Maggie Doyle, Nurse Takata (*ER*); Javier (*Felicity*); Susan, Carol (*Friends*); Brian (*The Larry Sanders Show*); Blaine, Antoine (*In Living Color*); Ricky Vasquez (*My So-Called Life*); Ron, Eric (*Northern Exposure*); Ross, Perry (*Party of Five*); everyone (*Queer as Folk*); Norman, Beth, Pedro, Sean, Dan, Arnie, Johnny, Genesis, Ruthie, Justin (*The Real World*); Leon, Nancy, Bev (*Roseanne*); Susan (*Seinfeld*); Stanford, Anthony (*Sex and the City*); Waylon Smithers, Patty Bouvier (*The Simpsons*); Big Gay Al (*South Park*); Rich (*Survivor*); Michael, Mona, Anna, Jon, Dorothy, Beauchamp, Peter, Charles (*Tales of the City*); David, William (*The Tracey Ullman Show*); Tinky Winky (*The Teletubbies*); Will Truman, Jack McFarland (*Will and Grace*); Xena (*Xena: Warrior Princess*)

"Make no mistake, America. We won't compromise our freedom. We won't go back. We will win."

—David B. Mixner, civil rights activist, at the 1993 March on Washington

This is no doubt just a partial list of lesbigay (that was a word occasionally used back then) characters being beamed into households in the 1990s.

But visibility and progress was seemingly everywhere. Melissa Etheridge came out. Comedy Central's *Out There* featured strictly gay stand-up comedians. Deborah Batts became the first openly lesbian federal judge. The Central Conference of American Rabbis (the oldest rabbinical organization in the world) declared all Jews to be "religiously equal regardless of their sexual orientation." And what

Opposite: Gilbert Baker's thirty-foot-wide Rainbow Flag stretches more than twenty blocks down Sixth Avenue (a *Guinness World Records* record holder at the time) in celebration of Stonewall's twenty-fifth anniversary, 1994.

is known as "the largest and most famous lesbian/queer girl party music festival in the world"—the Club Skirts Dinah Shore Weekend ("the Dinah")—came about thanks to a women's golf tournament after-party in Palm Springs. There were also gay magazines and film festivals and Olympic-style games and restaurants and bookstores and every possible kind of gay group you could dream up, from gay scuba divers to lesbian computer hackers.

And—for the first time ever in a presidential campaign—there were gay issues. "Gay Politics Goes Mainstream," announced the *New York Times Magazine* in the October 11, 1992 issue. "This is untested ground in a presidential race," the article said, reporting that "When it is suggested that his pro-gay positions might be political suicide, he [Democratic nominee Bill Clinton] shakes his head no. But then he bursts out laughing and says, 'Maybe.'"

In September 1992, on the ABC News program *This Week*, Republican vice presidential candidate Dan Quayle shared his thoughts on homosexuality: "My viewpoint is that it's more of a choice than a biological situation. I think it is a wrong choice." One hundred and ten gay delegates were on the floor at the Democratic National Convention; only two alternates represented the gay community at the Republican convention, where placards read FAMILY RIGHTS FOREVER/GAY RIGHTS NEVER. Signs in gay bookstores, bars, and churches across the country responded: VOTING FOR OUR LIVES.

So while strides were being made at an ever-accelerating pace culturally, politics was still debating, and pushback was fierce. "Don't Ask, Don't Tell" became the law of the land in 1994, allowing soldiers to serve only if they stayed locked tight in the closet. The Defense of Marriage Act in 1996 declared that "the word 'marriage' means only a legal union between one man and one woman as husband and wife, and the word 'spouse' refers only to a person of the opposite sex who is a husband or a wife."

But there was the astounding amount of positive coverage in the media. There was the 1993 march on Washington—one of the largest demonstrations in the history of the United States—demanding civil rights, the end of sodomy laws, inclusion in educational programs, AIDS education and research funding, the right to adopt, and an end to violent oppression. There were so many strides forward. And then there was Matthew Shepard. In October 1998, the twenty-one-year-old openly gay University of Wyoming student was beaten beyond recognition, tied to a log fence, and left for dead. Outside his funeral service, Fred Phelps and members of his fundamentalist Westboro Baptist Church picketed with hateful signs, the most noxious reading, GOD HATES FAGS.

Opposite: Ellen DeGeneres (right) with then girlfriend Anne Heche in 1997, shortly after her character Ellen Morgan came out in the Emmy-winning "The Puppy Episode" of her TV sitcom *Ellen*. **Above**: A spread from the US Army–issued comic book, *Dignity & Respect: A Training Guide on Homosexual Conduct Policy*, explaining how to deal with "Don't Ask, Don't Tell," 2001.

"As the world's largest sports and cultural event open to all, the Gay Games have created and nurtured a movement that has become among the greatest forces for community empowerment and social change. The Gay Games is open to all, young or old, athlete or artist, experienced or novice, gay or straight." —GayGames.org

Above: The opening ceremony at the Gay Games in New York City, June 1994. **Opposite**: Sonny Koerner (left) and Mark Larson, American athletes (competing in rodeo) at the opening ceremony of the Gay Games in Sydney, November 2, 2002.

Sonny
Mark

GAYS

WE ARE AFRAID NO MORE

Speech at the March on Washington for LGBT Rights, April 25, 1993

by Urvashi Vaid

Hello lesbian and gay Americans. I am proud to stand before you as a lesbian today. With hearts full of love and with an abiding faith in justice, we have come to Washington to speak to America.

We have come to speak the truth of our lives and silence the liars.

We have come to challenge the cowardly Congress to end its paralysis and exercise moral leadership.

We have come to defend our honor and win our equality.

But most of all, we have come in peace and with courage to say, "America, this day marks the return from exile of the gay and lesbian people."

We are banished no more.

We wander the wilderness of despair no more.

We are afraid no more.

For on this day, with love in our hearts, we have come out, to reach out across America to build a bridge of understanding, a bridge of progress, a bridge as solid as steel, a bridge to a land where no one suffers prejudice because of their sexual orientation, their race, their gender, their religion, or their human difference.

I've been asked by the march organizers to speak . . . about the Far Right, the Far Right which threatens the construction of this bridge. The extremist Right which has targeted every one of you and me for extinction, the supremacist Right which seeks to redefine the very meaning of democracy.

Language itself fails in this task, my friends, for to call our opponents "the Right" states a profound untruth. They are wrong. They are wrong.

Opposite: The first National March on Washington for Lesbian and Gay Rights, October 14, 1979. The second march, prompted by the lack of government attention to the AIDS epidemic, was held on October 11, 1987, and the third—one of the largest protests in American history—was on April 25, 1993.

They are wrong morally, they are wrong spiritually, and they are wrong politically.

The Christian supremacists are wrong spiritually when they demonize us. They are wrong when they reduce the complexity and beauty of our spirit into a freak show. They are wrong spiritually, because if we are the untouchables of America, then we are, as Mahatma Gandhi said, children of God. And as God's children we know that the gods of our understanding, the gods of goodness and love and righteousness, march right here with us today.

The supremacists who lead the anti-gay crusade are wrong morally. They are wrong because justice is moral, and prejudice is evil. Because truth is moral, and the lie of the closet is the real sin. Because their claim of morality is a simple subterfuge, a strategy that hides their real aim, which is much more secular. Christian supremacist leaders like Bill Bennett and Pat Robertson, Lou Sheldon and Pat Buchanan, supremacists like Phyllis Schlafly and Ralph Reed, Bill Kristol and R. J. Rushdoony—these supremacist leaders don't care about morality; they care about power. They care about social control. And their goal, my friends, is the reconstruction of American democracy into American theocracy. . . .

They say they have declared a cultural war on us. It's a war, all right. It's a war about values. On one side are the values that everyone here stands for . . . traditional American values of democracy and pluralism. On the other side are those who want to turn the Christian church into the government, those whose value is monotheism.

We believe in democracy—in many voices coexisting in peace, and people of all faiths living together in harmony under a common civil framework known as the United States Constitution.

Our opponents believe in monotheism—one way (theirs), one god (theirs), one law (the Old Testament), one nation supreme (the Christian, white one). . . .

Democracy battles theism in Oregon, in Colorado, in Florida, in Maine, in Arizona, in Michigan, in Ohio, in Idaho, in Washington, in Montana, in every state where you, my brothers and sisters, are leading the fight to oppose the Right and to defend the United States Constitution.

We won the anti-gay measure in Oregon, but today . . . thirty-three counties and municipalities face local versions of that ordinance The fight has just begun. We lost a big fight in Colorado, but thanks to the hard work of all the people of Colorado, the Boycott Colorado movement is working, and it's strong, and we're going to win our freedom there eventually.

To defeat the Right politically, my friends, is our challenge when we leave this march. How can we do it? We've got to march from Washington into action at home.

I challenge every one of you—straight or gay—who can hear my voice to join the national gay and lesbian movement. I challenge you to join NGLTF to fight the Right. We've got to match the power of the Christian supremacists member for member, vote for vote, dollar for dollar.

I challenge each of you to not just buy a T-shirt but get involved in your movement. Get involved. Volunteer. Volunteer. Every local organization in this country needs you. Every clinic, every hotline, every youth program needs you, needs your time and your love.

And I also challenge our straight liberal allies—liberals and libertarians, independents and conservatives, Republican or radical—I challenge and invite you to open your eyes and embrace us without fear.

The gay rights movement is not a party.

It is not lifestyle. It is not a hairstyle.

It is not a fad or a fringe or a sickness.

It is not about sin or salvation.

The gay rights movement is an integral part of the American promise of freedom.

We, you and I, each of us, we are the descendants of a proud tradition of people asserting our dignity.

It is fitting that the Holocaust Museum was dedicated the same weekend as this march, for not only were gay people persecuted by the Nazi state, but gay people are indebted to the struggle of the Jewish people against bigotry and intolerance.

It is fitting that the NAACP marches with us, that feminist leaders march with us, because we are indebted to those movements.

When all of us who believe in freedom and diversity see this gathering, we see beauty and power. When our enemies see this gathering, they see the millennium.

Well, perhaps the religious Right is [right] about something.

We call for the end of the world as we know it. We call for the end of racism and bigotry as we know it.

For the end of violence and discrimination and homophobia as we know it.

For the end of sexism as we know it.

We stand for freedom as we have yet to know it.

And we will not be denied.

Above: Urvashi Vaid, then the executive director of the National Gay and Lesbian Task Force (the country's oldest national LGBTQ advocacy group), interrupting a speech by President George H. W. Bush in Arlington, Virginia, March 29, 1990. Vaid is currently CEO of The Vaid Group LLC, a social innovation firm that works with global and domestic organizations to advance equity, justice, and inclusion.

"Sometimes we are blessed with being able to choose the time and the arena and the manner of our revolution, but more usually we must do battle wherever we are standing."

—Audre Lorde, self-described "black, lesbian, mother, warrior, poet"

Above: Two couples at the New York City Dyke March, which takes place each year on the Saturday before the Pride parade to demonstrate for lesbian rights and visibility, June 24, 1995. **Opposite**: The Gay Pride Parade (Marche des Fiertés LGBT), Paris, France, c. 1995.

Contrat d'Union Sociale
Nous nous aimons nous le voulons !
CHASSE A L'HOMME
36.68.32.3
CODE 2021
48.33.38.07
LE MANS POUR LE C.U.S.

Above: Elizabeth Taylor (left) and Elton John at Madison Square Garden in New York at the first concert benefiting the Elizabeth Taylor AIDS Foundation, October 11, 1992. **Opposite**: Olympic diver Greg Louganis at the Los Angeles Summer Olympics in 1992. He spoke publicly for the first time about being gay and HIV-positive in a 1995 interview with Barbara Walters on *Good Morning America*.

US

BRAVE

REAL CHANGE
(The 21st Century)

In June 2003, almost thirty-four years to the day after Stonewall, the Supreme Court of the United States of America voted to make gay sex legal—6 to 3. The majority opinion written by Justice Anthony Kennedy says in part, "The question before the Court is the validity of a Texas statute making it a crime for two persons of the same sex to engage in certain intimate sexual conduct. In Houston, Texas, officers of the Harris County Police Department were dispatched to a private residence in response to a reported weapons disturbance. They entered an apartment where one of the petitioners, John Geddes Lawrence, resided.... The officers observed Lawrence and another man, Tyron Garner, engaging in a sexual act. The two petitioners were arrested, held in custody over night, and charged and convicted before a Justice of the Peace."

This story seems almost absurd today.

With the help of the civil rights organization Lambda Legal they appealed the decision all the way to the Supreme Court, which concluded, "The petitioners are entitled to respect for their private lives. The state cannot demean their existence or control their destiny by making their private sexual conduct a crime.... Times can blind us to certain

"The whole perception of sexual orientation is being challenged by the millennials. Among the cohort of 12-to-19-year-olds defining Generation Z, the lines between male and female are becoming increasingly blurred."

—Lucie Greene, worldwide director, JWT Intelligence

Opposite: Gender nonconforming supermodel Avie Acosta, Milan, 2018.

truths and later generations can see that laws once thought necessary and proper in fact serve only to oppress. As the Constitution endures, persons in every generation can invoke its principles in their own search for greater freedom."

Justice Antonin Scalia disagreed. "Many Americans do not want persons who openly engage in homosexual conduct as partners in their business, as scoutmasters for their children, as teachers in their children's schools, or as boarders in their home," he wrote. "In most states what the Court calls 'discrimination' against those who engage in homosexual acts is perfectly legal."

But he was on the losing side of the argument. And as the twenty-first century gets under way, discrimination, legal and otherwise, continues to fall by the wayside. In December 2010, "Don't Ask, Don't Tell" was repealed. In January 2013, President Barack Obama became the first US president to use the word *gay* in an inaugural speech. In June 2015, marriage was declared legal for everyone in every state. In July 2015, the Boy Scouts lifted the ban on gay leaders. In June 2016, Stonewall became a national monument. In August 2016, fifty-five openly LGBTQ+ athletes competed at the Olympics in Rio. In November 2016, openly bisexual Kate Brown was elected governor

of Oregon. In June 2017, Washington, DC, drivers were given the option of "X" as gender on their license. And in November 2017, Virginia sent transgender candidate Danica Roem to their state legislature. And the century is only in its teenage years.

Yes, in July 2017, President Trump tweeted that trans folks were not welcome in the military, and around the world many LGBTQ+ people are still persecuted and still live in hiding and fear. But one hundred years after the Harlem Renaissance, seventy-five years after the sea change brought about by World War II, and fifty years after the patrons of a small bar on Christopher Street rebelled, the clear trend is pointing toward rights and freedom. The beliefs and attitudes that stoke sexual prejudice—beliefs entrenched for so long in society—often die hard. As James Baldwin wrote in the 1950s, "Any real change implies the breakup of the world as one has always known it."

Opposite: Protesters march at the Justice Department in response to the suicide of transgender teenager Leelah Alcorn, 2015.
Above: Gay rights supporters in West Hollywood celebrating the repeal of the "Don't Ask, Don't Tell" policy that negatively affected nearly 15,000 service members, September 20, 2011.

WE'RE HERE, MR. PRESIDENT, ENLIST US NOW!

Remarks by President Barack Obama at the Signing of the Don't Ask, Don't Tell Repeal Act of 2010, Washington, DC, December 22, 2010 [abridged]

Sixty-six years ago, in the dense, snow-covered forests of Western Europe, Allied forces were beating back a massive assault in what would become known as the Battle of the Bulge. And in the final days of fighting, a regiment in the 80th Division of Patton's Third Army came under fire. The men were traveling along a narrow trail. They were exposed and they were vulnerable. Hundreds of soldiers were cut down by the enemy.

And during the firefight, a private named Lloyd Corwin tumbled forty feet down the deep side of a ravine. And dazed and trapped, he was as good as dead. But one soldier, a friend, turned back. And with shells landing around him, amid smoke and chaos and the screams of wounded men, this soldier, this friend, scaled down the icy slope, risking his own life to bring Private Corwin to safer ground.

For the rest of his years, Lloyd credited this soldier, this friend, named Andy Lee, with saving his life, knowing he would never have made it out alone. It was a full four decades after the war, when the two friends reunited in their golden years, that Lloyd learned that the man who saved his life, his friend Andy, was gay. He had no idea. And he didn't much care. Lloyd knew what mattered. He knew what had kept him alive, what made it possible for him to come home and start a family and live the rest of his life. It was his friend.

And Lloyd's son is with us today. And he knew that valor and sacrifice are no more limited by sexual orientation than they are by race or by gender or by religion or by creed, that what made it possible for him to survive the battlefields of Europe is the reason that we are here today. That's the reason we are here today.

So this morning, I am proud to sign a law that will bring an end to "Don't Ask, Don't Tell." . . . No longer will our country be denied the service of thousands of patriotic Americans who were forced to leave the military—regardless of their skills, no matter their bravery or their zeal, no matter their years of exemplary

Opposite: Sgt. Brandon Morgan (right) embracing his partner, Dalan Wells, at the Marine base in Kaneohe, Hawaii, February 2012.

performance—because they happen to be gay. No longer will tens of thousands of Americans in uniform be asked to live a lie, or look over their shoulder, in order to serve the country that they love.

As Admiral Mike Mullen has said, "Our people sacrifice a lot for their country, including their lives. None of them should have to sacrifice their integrity as well."

That's why I believe this is the right thing to do for our military. That's why I believe it is the right thing to do, period. . . .

I want to express my gratitude to the men and women in this room who have worn the uniform of the United States Armed Services. I want to thank all the patriots who are here today, all of them who were forced to hang up their uniforms as a result of "Don't Ask, Don't Tell"—but who never stopped fighting for this country, and who rallied and who marched and fought for change. I want to thank everyone here who stood with them in that fight.

Because of these efforts, in the coming days we will begin the process laid out by this law. Now, the old policy remains in effect until Secretary Gates, Admiral Mullen, and I certify the military's readiness to implement the repeal. And it's especially important for service members to remember that. But I have spoken to every one of the service chiefs, and they are all committed to implementing this change swiftly and efficiently. We are not going to be dragging our feet to get this done. . . .

I am certain that we can effect this transition in a way that only strengthens our military readiness, that people will look back on this moment and wonder why it was ever a source of controversy in the first place.

I have every confidence in the professionalism and patriotism of our service members. Just as they have adapted and grown stronger with each of the other changes, I know they will do so again. I know that Secretary Gates, Admiral Mullen, as well as the vast majority of service members themselves share this view. And they share it based on their own experiences, including the experience of serving with dedicated, duty-bound service members who were also gay.

As one special operations warfighter said during the Pentagon's review—this was one of my favorites—it echoes the experience of Lloyd Corwin decades earlier: "We have a gay guy in the unit. He's big, he's mean, he kills lots of bad guys. No one cared that he was gay." And I think that sums up perfectly the situation.

Finally, I want to speak directly to the gay men and women currently serving in our military. For a long time your service has demanded a particular kind of sacrifice. You've been asked to carry the added burden of secrecy and isolation. And all the while, you've put your lives on the line for the freedoms and privileges of citizenship that are not fully granted to you. You're not the first to have carried this burden, for while today marks the end of a particular struggle that has lasted almost two decades, this is a moment more than two centuries in the making.

There will never be a full accounting of the heroism demonstrated by gay Americans in service to this country; their service has been obscured in history. It's been lost to prejudices that have waned in our own lifetimes. But at every turn, every crossroads in our past, we know gay Americans fought just as hard, gave

There can be little doubt there were gay soldiers who fought for American independence, who consecrated the ground at Gettysburg, who manned the trenches along the Western Front, who stormed the beaches of Iwo Jima.

just as much to protect this nation and the ideals for which it stands.

There can be little doubt there were gay soldiers who fought for American independence, who consecrated the ground at Gettysburg, who manned the trenches along the Western Front, who stormed the beaches of Iwo Jima. Their names are etched into the walls of our memorials. Their headstones dot the grounds at Arlington.

And so, as the first generation to serve openly in our Armed Forces, you will stand for all those who came before you, and you will serve as role models to all who come after. And I know that you will fulfill this responsibility with integrity and honor, just as you have every other mission with which you've been charged.

And you need to look no further than the servicemen and women in this room—distinguished officers like former Navy Commander Zoe Dunning. Marines like Eric Alva, one of the first Americans to be injured in Iraq. Leaders like Captain Jonathan Hopkins, who led a platoon into northern Iraq during the initial invasion, quelling an ethnic riot, earning a Bronze Star with valor. He was discharged, only to receive emails and letters from his soldiers saying they had known he was gay all along and thought that he was the best commander they ever had.

There are a lot of stories like these—stories that only underscore the importance of enlisting the service of all who are willing to fight for this country. That's why I hope those soldiers, sailors, airmen, Marines, and Coast Guardsmen who have been discharged under this discriminatory policy will seek to reenlist once the repeal is implemented.

That is why I say to all Americans, gay or straight, who want nothing more than to defend this country in uniform: Your country needs you, your country wants you, and we will be honored to welcome you into the ranks of the finest military the world has ever known.

For we are not a nation that says, "don't ask, don't tell." We are a nation that says, "Out of many, we are one." We are a nation that welcomes the service of every patriot. We are a nation that believes that all men and women are created equal. Those are the ideals that generations have fought for. Those are the ideals that we uphold today. And now, it is my honor to sign this bill into law.

AUDIENCE MEMBER: Thank you, Mr. President!

THE PRESIDENT: Thank you!

AUDIENCE MEMBER: We're here, Mr. President. Enlist us now.

"The world changes in direct proportion to the number of people willing to be honest about their lives."

—Armistead Maupin

Above: Over 60,000 participants at the Taipei Gay Pride parade in Taiwan, the largest gay celebration in Asia, October 2015. **Opposite**: Celebrating at Toronto's Trans March, June 2012. **Following pages**: The White House, lit in rainbow colors, the night the Supreme Court ruled on marriage equality, June 26, 2015.

Rexall
Rexall
NOVACKS

01-05245-2015
United in Marriage
To any person authorized by the laws of the State of Texas to conduct marriage ceremonies in the State of Texas:
STATE OF TEXAS
County of Travis
You are hereby authorized to celebrate the
Rites of Matrimony
between
Javier Vera Suarez and Gerardo Vela Arines
MR

MARRIAGE EQUALITY

Obergefell v. Hodges, US Supreme Court decision, June 26, 2015 [extract]

The Constitution promises liberty to all within its reach, a liberty that includes certain specific rights that allow persons, within a lawful realm, to define and express their identity. The petitioners in these cases seek to find that liberty by marrying someone of the same sex and having their marriages deemed lawful on the same terms and conditions as marriages between persons of the opposite sex. . . .

The ancient origins of marriage confirm its centrality, but it has not stood in isolation from developments in law and society. The history of marriage is one of both continuity and change. That institution—even as confined to opposite-sex relations—has evolved over time. . . . These new insights have strengthened, not weakened, the institution of marriage. . . .

The right to marry is fundamental as a matter of history and tradition, but rights come not from ancient sources alone. They rise, too, from a better informed understanding of how constitutional imperatives define a liberty that remains urgent in our own era. . . . Under the Constitution, same-sex couples seek in marriage the same legal treatment as opposite-sex couples, and it would disparage their choices and diminish their personhood to deny them this right. . . .

No union is more profound than marriage, for it embodies the highest ideals of love, fidelity, devotion, sacrifice, and family. In forming a marital union, two people become something greater than once they were. As some of the petitioners in these cases demonstrate, marriage embodies a love that may endure even past death. It would misunderstand these men and women to say they disrespect the idea of marriage. Their plea is that they do respect it, respect it so deeply that they seek to find its fulfillment for themselves. Their hope is not to be condemned to live in loneliness, excluded from one of civilization's oldest institutions. They ask for equal dignity in the eyes of the law. The Constitution grants them that right.

Opposite: One of dozens of happy couples during a mass wedding ceremony a week after the US Supreme Court's landmark marriage equality decision, Austin, Texas, July 2015.

RESIST
RESIST

"This week I'm designating the Stonewall National Monument as the newest addition to America's National Park System. Stonewall will be our first national monument to tell the story of the struggle for LGBT rights. I believe our national parks should reflect the full story of our country, the richness and diversity and uniquely American spirit that has always defined us. That we are stronger together. That out of many, we are one." —President Barack Obama, June 2016

Opposite: Protesters rally following President Trump's tweets announcing a ban on transgender people serving in the military, July 2017. **Above**: The Stonewall Inn and Sheridan Square became a national monument in June 2016.

“Unfortunately . . . there are still countries in which homosexuality is persecuted, sometimes even by jail sentences, and in which the rainbow flag is forbidden. Russia is one of these countries.”

—Federación Estatal de Lesbianas, Gais, Trans, y Bisexuales (FELGTB)

Opposite: Defying a government ban on “gay propaganda,” six brave LGBT activists stroll through Moscow’s Red Square using their countries’ football team jerseys to form a human gay flag. The #HIDDENFLAG group—(from left to right) Marta Márquez (Spain), Eric Houter (The Netherlands), Eloi Pierozan Junior (Brazil), Guillermo León (Mexico), Vanesa Paola Ferrario (Argentina), and Mateo Fernández Gómez (Colombia)—visited iconic sites in Russia during the 2018 World Cup in support of their repressed gay brothers and sisters.

BRASIL
10
adidas
AFA
adidas

DUPLEX

"All of us who are openly gay are living and writing the history of our movement. We are no more—and no less—heroic than the suffragists and abolitionists of the nineteenth century; and the labor organizers, Freedom Riders, Stonewall demonstrators, and environmentalists of the twentieth century. We are ordinary people, living our lives, and trying, as civil rights activist Dorothy Cotton said, to 'fix what ain't right' in our society."

—Senator Tammy Baldwin

Opposite: Hundreds gather in front of the Stonewall Inn to hear speakers at a memorial for those killed at the Pulse nightclub in Orlando, Florida, the deadliest incident of violence against LGBT people in US history, New York, June 13, 2016.

ACKNOWLEDGMENTS

Sterling Publishing is grateful to book producer Esther Margolis of Newmarket Publishing Management Corporation, who deftly oversaw this book's production and as always was unflappable and steadfast even during the most demanding of schedules. We are also thankful to author Christopher Measom of Night & Day Design for his insightful text as well as his impeccable and deeply dedicated photo editing and research—along with his partner, Timothy Shaner, who brings the highest level of excellence and elevated design sensibility to every project. We are grateful to them all for their enthusiasm and expertise.

Esther Margolis, Christopher Measom, and Timothy Shaner wish to acknowledge the following:

For their assistance with image and text contributions to our book—thanks to Jonathan Silin of the Robert Giard estate, photographer Joan E. Biren (JEB) for her unique and lovely portraits, Richard Schneider at the *Gay & Lesbian Review* for his patience and generosity providing the fascinating Edmund White and Michael Denneny remembrances, and the indomitable Larry Kramer for approving the use of extracts from his groundbreaking play *The Normal Heart*.

For their dedication preserving, sharing, and enabling our access to this amazing history, we are especially grateful to Caitlin McCarthy at the LGBT Community Center Archives in New York, Loni Shibuyama at the *One* Archives (part of the USC Libraries in Los Angeles), Patricia Delara at the GLBT Historical Society in San Francisco, and Susan Goldstein at the San Francisco Public Library.

For their editorial contributions and wordsmithing advice, we thank independent editors Antonia Felix, Lori Paximadis, and Wilda Williams; and, of course, the amazing team at Sterling Publishing—Christine Heun, art director, interiors; Elizabeth Lindy, senior art director, covers and cover designer; Christopher Bain, photography director; Fred Pagan, production manager; and especially executive editor Barbara Berger, whose expert guidance, keen eye, and unflagging support helped to bring everything together so beautifully.

NOTES

INTRODUCTION

PAGE 1: **"We were dancing":** *The Death and Life of Marsha P. Johnson*, directed by David France, 2017. **"The world was so different":** *Pay It No Mind: Marsha P. Johnson*, directed by Michael Kasino, 2012. **"The police got the shock":** Charles Kaiser, *The Gay Metropolis: 1940–1996* (New York: Houghton Mifflin Company, 1997), 200.

PAGE 2: **"In the 1950s . . .":** Brief of amici curiae historians of antigay discrimination in support of plaintiffs-appellees, case nos. 14-1167(l), 14-1169, 14-1173, United States Court of Appeals for the Fourth Circuit, 9. **"US Senate declared":** Hoey Committee Report, Employment of Homosexuals and Other Sex Perverts in Government (records of the US Senate, RG 46), 19.

PAGE 3: **"Just please let there be," "We were scared":** *Stonewall Uprising: The Year That Changed America*, directed by Kate Davis and David Heilbroner, *American Experience*, PBS, April 25, 2011.

PAGE 5: **"the distinction between":** Andrew Sullivan, "The End of Gay Culture," *The New Republic*, October 24, 2005.

PART 1: WE'RE HERE . . .

PAGE 9: **"was surely as gay":** Linda Villarosa, "The Gay Harlem Renaissance," TheRoot.com, July 23, 2011. **"people with taste":** Caroline F. Ware, *Greenwich Village, 1920–1930* (Los Angeles: University of California Press, 1963), 19. **"specifically casting gay men":** Geoff Cobb, "Mae West's Gay Drama That Shocked 1920s America," Greenpointers.com, November 14, 2018.

PAGE 10: **"editorial calling it 'immoral'":** James Douglas, "A Book That Must Be Supressed," *Sunday Express*, August 19, 1928. **"sexologist Magnus Hirschfeld":** Ralf Dose, *Magnus Hirschfeld: The Origins of the Gay Liberation Movement* (New York: Monthly Review Press, 2014), 59. **"promote and protect," "planted a powder puff":** Marc Stein, *Rethinking the Gay and Lesbian Movement* (New York: Routledge, 2012), 37, 38. **"hated traditional girl tasks":** "Reminiscences of Hall's Summit," *Hall's Summit News*, June 10, 1921.

PAGE 14: **"independent yet feminine":** Charlotte Herzog, "A Rose by Any Other Name: Violet Oakley, Jessie Wilcox Smith, and Elizabeth Shippen Green," *Women's Art Journal* (Autumn 1993–Winter 1994): 11–16.

PAGE 16: **"Good friend and interior":** Eve Golden, *Golden Images: 41 Essays on Silent Film Stars* (Jefferson, NC: McFarland and Company, 2001), 45.

PAGE 22: **"a large, dark masculine lady":** Steven J. Niven, "Blues Singer Gladys Bentley Broke Ground with Marriage to a Woman in 1931," TheRoot.com, February 11, 2015. **"strayed from," "a woman again":** Gladys Bentley, "I Am a Woman Again," *Ebony*, August 1952. **"one of the rankest":** James F. Wilson, *Bulldaggers, Pansies, and Chocolate Babies* (Ann Arbor: University of Michigan Press, 2010), 156.

PAGE 29: **"more than 16 million Americans":** US Department of Veterans Affairs, "America's Wars," May 2017, va.gov/opa/publications/factsheets/fs_americas_wars.pdf. **"Everybody was released":** Charles Kaiser, *Gay Metropolis: 1940–1996* (New York: Houghton Mifflin, 1997), 40. **"The war made me":** Sherna Berger Gluck, *Rosie the Riveter Revisited: Women, the War, and Social Change* (New York: Penguin Group, 1988), 23. **"I was resolved that our women":** Robert Lopresti, *When Women Didn't Count* (Santa Barbara, CA: ABC-CLIO, 2017), 241.

PAGE 30: **"The combination":** Charles Kaiser, *Gay Metropolis: 1940–1996* (New York: Houghton Mifflin, 1997), 27.

PAGE 41: **"what historian Joan Nestle":** Morgan Gwenwald, "Queer Covers: From Lesbian Survival Literature," Lesbian Herstory Archives, newsletter 15, January 1995. **"I knew the government":** Stuart Timmons, *The Trouble with Harry Hay: Founder of the Modern Gay Movement* (New York: Alyson Publications, 1990), 135. **"At least 37 percent":** Alfred C. Kinsey, Wardell R. Pomeroy, and Clyde E. Martin, *Sexual Behavior in the Human Male* (Bloomington: Indiana University Press, 1948), 623.

PAGE 42: **"We knew we were outside":** Charles Kaiser, *Gay Metropolis: 1940–1996* (New York: Houghton Mifflin, 1997), 86. **"The privilege of working":** Judith Adkins, "These People Are Frightened to Death: Congressional Investigations and the Lavender Scare," *Prologue Magazine*, Summer 2016. **"1.2 million":** The National WWII Museum, "African Americans in World War II: Fighting for Double Victory," nationalww2museum.org/sites/default/files/2017-07/african-americans.pdf. **"educate homosexuals," "a woman's organization":** Jonathan Katz, *Gay American History: Lesbians and Gay Men in the USA* (New York: Thomas Y. Crowell, 1976), 412.

PAGE 44: **"We didn't start":** Chloe Hadjimatheou, "Christine Jorgensen: 60 Years of Sex Change Ops," BBC.com, November 30, 2012. **"Cold War–era feminine ideal":** Emily Skidmore, "Constructing the 'Good Transsexual': Christine Jorgensen, Whiteness, and Heteronormativity in the Mid-Twentieth-Century Press," *Feminist Studies* 37, no. 2 (2011). **Frail, introverted:** Associated Press, "Famed Transsexual Christine Jorgensen Out of the Spotlight," *Los Angeles Times*, June 22, 1986. **"A woman trapped":** *The Christine Jorgensen Story*, directed by Irving Rapper, 1970. **"Nature made":** Ben White, "Ex GI Becomes Blonde Beauty," *New York Daily News*, December 1, 1952. **"Well-filled":** International News Service, "New Career Is Begun by Christine Jorgensen," *Cincinnati Enquirer*, February 12, 1953.

PAGE 48: **"We are an oppressed":** Lillian Faderman, *The Gay Revolution: The Story of the Struggle* (New York: Simon and Schuster, 2015), 57. **"One of the seminal," "dignified and useful," "the terror":** Harry Hay, *Radically Gay: Gay Liberation in the Words of Its Founder*, ed. Will Roscoe (Boston: Beacon Press, 1996), 130, 131, 170.

PAGE 53: **"isolated and separated . . . self-esteem":** Phyllis Lyon, "Lesbian Liberation Begins," *Gay & Lesbian Review*, (Vol. 100, November–December 2012). **"More radical":** Robert Aldrich, *Gay Lives* (New York: Thames and Hudson, 2012), 246.

PART 2: WE'RE QUEER . . .

PAGE 59: **"turning donuts":** Lillian Faderman, *The Gay Revolution: The Story of the Struggle* (New York: Simon and Schuster, 2015), 116. **"We as liberated":** Julie Bolcer, "Arthur Evans, Cofounder of Gay Activists Alliance, Dies at 68," Advocate.com, September 15, 2011. **"Without our demonstrations":** Michael G. Long, *Gay Is Good: The Life and Letters of Gay Rights Pioneer Franklin Kameny* (Syracuse, NY: Syracuse University Press, 2014), 194.

PAGE 60: **"We got tired":** *Screaming Queens: The Riot at Compton's Cafeteria*, directed by Victor Silverman and Susan Stryker, 2005. **"at the Waikiki bar," "the court ruled":** Jim Farber, "Before the Stonewall Uprising, There Was the 'Sip-In,'" *New York Times*, April 20, 2016. **"Two males kissing":** Leo Duran, "Stonewall Riots Grab the Spotlight from Black Cat Protests," *Morning Edition*, NPR, February 13, 2017. **"There was no going back":** *Stonewall Uprising: The Year That Changed America*, directed by Kate Davis and David Heilbroner, *American Experience*, April 25, 2011. **"The Stonewall uprising":** Dennis Hevesi, "Seymour Pine Dies at 91; Led Raid on Stonewall Inn," *New York Times*, September 7, 2010.

PAGE 78: **"butch lesbian":** Trish Bendix, "Will *Stonewall* and *Suffragette* Leave Queer Women Out of History?" AfterEllen.com, August 5, 2015. **"long-time friend":** William Yardley, "Stormé DeLarverie, Early Leader in Gay Rights Movement, Dies at 93," *New York Times*, May 29, 2014. **"was jumping on":** *A Stormé Life*, video, itlmedia, June 30, 2009, youtube.com/watch?v=XgCVNEiOwLs. **"Nobody knows":** William Yardley, "Stormé DeLarverie, Early Leader in Gay Rights Movement, Dies at 93," *New York Times*, May 29, 2014.

PAGE 80: **"Those early pickets":** *Gay Pioneers*, directed by Glenn Holsten, 2001.

PAGE 83: **"a flyer appeared":** Donn Teal, *The Gay Militants* (New York: Stein and Day, 1971), 36. **"well over a thousand":** Stephen M. Engel, *The Unfinished Revolution: Social Movement Theory and the Gay and Lesbian Movement* (Cambridge: Cambridge University Press, 2001), 45. **"basic human rights":** Toby Marotta, *The Politics of Homosexuality* (New York: Houghton Mifflin, 1981), 159.

PAGE 84: **"End Police Harassment":** Tristan Poehlmann, *The Stonewall Riots: The Fight for LGBT Rights* (Mankato, MN: Essential Library, 2010), 83. **"The room is filled":** Charles Silverstein, "Events in New York City Leading to the Deletion of Homosexuality as a Mental Disorder by the American Psychiatric Association," *Division 44 Newsletter*, Spring 2011. **"We're becoming militant":** Lacey Fosburgh, "Thousands of Homosexuals Hold a Protest Rally in Central Park," *New York Times*, June 29, 1970. **"10 million":** *An American Family*, PBS, 1973, pbs.org/program/american-family.

PAGE 94: **"I was a no one," "could be perceived":** Sewell Chan, "Marsha P. Johnson: A Transgender Pioneer and Activist Who Was a Fixture of Greenwich Village Street Life," *New York Times*, March 8, 2018. **"Darling I want":** *After Stonewall*, directed by John Scagliotti, 1999. **"for the street gay people":** "Leslie Feinberg Interviews Sylvia Rivera" WorkersWorld.org, 1998. **"a bunch of flakey":** Eric Marcus, "Marsha P. Johnson and Randy Wicker," *Making Gay History: The Podcast*, May 2018.

PAGE 96: **"Before I die":** Sylvia Rivera, "Queens in Exile the Forgotten Ones," *Street Transvestite Action Revolutionaries: Survival, Revolt, and Queer Antagonist Struggle* (N.p.: Untorelli Press, 2013), 55.

PAGE 103: **"After I ran":** W. E. Barns, "An 'Unofficial Supervisor' Gets a Shot at Real Power," *San Francisco Examiner*, November 30, 1977. **"conspiracy of silence":** Harvey Milk Foundation, "Official Biography of Harvey Milk," MilkFoundation.org. **"If a bullet":** Ibid.

PAGE 107: **"Popular culture":** Andrew Sullivan, "The End of Gay Culture," *The New Republic*, October 24, 2005.

PAGE 108: **"What made us soar":** *After Stonewall*, directed by John Scagliotti, 1999.

PART 3: . . . GET USED TO IT!

PAGE 113: **"Rare cancer":** Lawrence K. Altman, "Rare Cancer Seen in 41 Homosexuals," *New York Times*, July 3, 1981. **"gay invisibility":** Charles Kaiser, *Gay Metropolis: 1940–1996* (New York: Houghton Mifflin Company, 1997), 269.

PAGE 115: **"We have to start":** *Vito*, directed by Jeffrey Schwarz , 2011. **"the most effective health activist":** Maia Szalavitz, "How to Survive a Plague: Q&A with ACT-UP's Peter Staley on Effective Activism," *Time*, September 27, 2012. **"highly skilled":** Zaahira Wyne, "The Women Who Fought AIDS: 'It Was Never Not Our Battle,'" Broadly.Vice.com, August 28, 2015. **"more than tripled":** Scott C. Ratzan, *AIDS: Effective Health Communication for the 90s* (London: Routledge, 2013), 143.

PAGE 121: **"Life is full of," "No matter how . . . That was my turning point":** *Vito*, directed by Jeffrey Schwarz, 2011.

PAGE 122: **"The whole industry," "most effective health activists":** Maia Szalavitz, "How to Survive a Plague: Q&A with ACT-UP's Peter Staley on Effective Activism," *Time*, September 27, 2012. **"We have people":** John Leland, "Twilight of a Difficult Man," *New York Times*, May 19, 2017.

PAGE 125: **"kill it by its throat":** *Larry King Live*, CNN, January 15, 2001.

PAGE 126: **"I could see it":** Xtra, "Cleve Jones on Harvey Milk and AIDS Memorial Quilt," November 29, 2011, youtube.com/watch?v=fEObIgSXtBY. **"More than 48,000 panels":** The Names Project, AIDSQuilt.org.

PAGE 131: **"religiously equal regardless":** Central Conference of American Rabbis, Resolution on Same Gender Officiation adopted at the 111th Convention of the Central Conference of American Rabbis, March 2000.

PAGE 133: **"largest demonstrations":** Nadine Smith, "The 20th Anniversary of the LGBT March on Washington: How Far Have We Come," HuffingtonPost.com, April 25, 2013.

PAGE 140: **"Sometimes we are":** Audre Lorde, *I Am Your Sister: Collected and Unpublished Writings of Audre Lorde*, eds. Rudolph P. Byrd, Johnnetta Betsch Cole, and Beverly Guy-Sheftall (New York: Oxford University Press, 2008), 140.

PAGE 145: **"The question before":** *Lawrence v. Texas*, Opinion, oyez.org, June 26, 2003. **"The whole perception," "the petitioners":** Ruth La Ferla, "In Fashion, Gender Lines Are Blurring," *New York Times*, August 19, 2015.

PAGE 146: **"Many Americans":** *Lawrence v. Texas*, Opinion, oyez.org, June 26, 2003. **"actually said":** "Inaugural Address by President Barack Obama," January 21, 2013, obamawhitehouse.archives.gov. **"marriage was declared":** *Obergefell v. Hodges*, oyez.org, June 26, 2015. **"fifty-five openly":** Outsports, "A Record 56 Out LBGT Athletes Compete in Rio Olympics," outsports.com, July 11, 2016.

PAGE 147: **"Trump tweeted":** Twitter post, @realDonaldTrump, July 26, 2017, 8:55 a.m., 9:04 a.m., 9:08 a.m. **"Any real change":** James Baldwin, *Nobody Knows My Name* (New York: Vintage Books, 1961), 117.

PAGE 152: **"The world changes":** Hermione Hoby, "Armistead Maupin: San Francisco's Chronicler Calls Time on His Saga," *The Guardian*, January 4, 2014.

PAGE 158: **"This week":** Barack Obama, "Weekly Address: Designating Stonewall National Monument," June 25, 2016, obamawhitehouse.archives.gov.

PAGE 160: **"Unfortunately":** TheHiddenFlag.org.

PAGE 163: **"All of us":** Tammy Baldwin, "Leaning toward Justice," *Windy City Times* (Chicago), October 3, 2007.

PICTURE CREDITS

Academy of Motion Picture Arts and Sciences, Margaret Herrick Library: 11

Alamy: Everett Collection: 35, 38; Mauritius images GmbH: 37; ZUMA Press: 147

Associated Press: J. Scott Applewhite: 123; Dennis Cook: 139; Wally Fong: 125; Mark Lennihan: 116; David Lewis: 148; Jacquelyn Martin: 81; John Redman: 124; Eric Risberg: 126

Beinecke Rare Book and Manuscript Library, Yale University: Robert Giard photograph © Jonathan Silin: 49, 52; Carl Van Vechten photograph © Van Vechten Trust: 23, 47, Peter Hujar Archives, 82

© **Joan E. Biren (JEB):** 78

Avram Finkelstein: 112, 114. 122

The GLBT Historical Society, San Francisco: Crawford Barton Papers: 104–105; Helen Harder Papers: 30; Courtesy of *Screaming Queens: The Riot at Compton's Cafeteria*: 3

Getty Images: Evan Agostini/Liaison: 140; Michael Abramson/The LIFE Images Collection: 119; Mladen Antonov: 154–155; Al Bello: 134; Martin Bernetti/AFP: ii–iii; Bettmann Archive: 25, 44, 50, 51, 64, 65, 84, 85, 128–129; Corbis: 36; Robert Daemmrich: 158; Larry Downing/Sygma: 132; Patrick Durand: 141; Fairfax Media Archive: 121; Craig Ferguson/Lightrocket: 152; Focus On Sport: 143; Fox Photos: 17; Allen Ginsberg: 46; Jeffrey Greenberg: 159; Jim Heimann Collection: 28; Natalia Herrero/iStock: 110–111; Hulton Archive: 17, 39, 43; John Kobal: 16; LightRocket: 158; Roberto Machado Noa/Lightrocket: 153; Yigal Mann/Michael Ochs Archives: 86–87; Kevin Mazur/WireImage: 142; Fred W. McDarrah: 56–57, 66–67, 69, 70; David McNew: iv–v; Viviane Moos: 130; Sonia Moskowitz: 107; Moviepix: 14; NY Daily News: 45, 68–69; The New York Post/Louis Liotta: 40; Bill O'Leary/The Washington Post: 146; Spencer Platt: 162–163; Popperfoto: 109; I.C. Rapoport: 62–63; Mark Reinstein: 136; Universal Images Group: 115; Grey Villet/The LIFE Picture Collection: 92–93; Angela Weiss/AFP: 144; Greg Wood: 135

© **Keith Haring Foundation** (artwork and writing): 4

The LGBT Community Center Archive, New York: Leonard Fink Photographs: viii, 88–89, 97 Visual Collection, box 5/folder 58: 6–7; Richard C. Wandel Photographs Collection: 58; Rudy Grillo Collection: 90, 91, 96

Library of Congress: 24, 26–27, 31, 33, 108, Carol Highsmith: 127, Alfred Palmer: 34

Navy Art Gallery/Paul Cadmus: 26–27

New York Public Library: 8, 12–13, 20, 79

Courtesy Netflix: 95

Dan Nicoletta: 98, 103

Oakland Museum of California: Bruce Reifel: 85

ONE Archives at the University of Southern California: 48; 54, 55, 80, 81, 113;

Private Collection: 15, 74 (*Boys in the Band* book cover, UK 1st Edition, Leo and Diane Dillon Illustration), 112, 114, 112

Rhino Entertainment Company: © Garry Gay: 106

Smithsonian: 14, 22, 61

Javier Tles/LOLA MullenLowe: 160–161

University of North Texas Libraries, Digital Library: 33, 39

US Army, Assistant Secretary for Manpower and Reserve Affairs: 133

Wikimedia Commons: 18, 19, 21(both), 32, 49, 53